THE LAW OF
MICRONATIONS

Constitutions, Codes, Treaties, and Other Documents
from Micronational Legislation and Jurisprudence

2018 EDITION

Compiled by the people of the Cyanocitta Isopod's Republic

Contents

Introduction

"A micronation, sometimes referred to as a model country or new country project, is an entity that claims to be an independent nation or state but is not recognized by world governments or major international organizations.

Micronations are distinguished from imaginary countries and from other kinds of social groups...by expressing a formal and persistent, even if unrecognized, claim of sovereignty over some physical territory. Micronations are also distinct from true secessionist movements; micronations' activities are almost always trivial enough to be ignored rather than challenged by the established nations whose territory they claim...

...The earliest known micronations date from the beginning of the 19th century. The advent of the Internet provided the means for people to create many new micronations, whose members are scattered all over the world and interact mostly by electronic means, often calling their nations "nomadic countries"...

...Micronations generally have a number of common features, although these may vary widely. They may have a structure similar to established sovereign states, including territorial claims, government institutions, official symbols and citizens, albeit on a much smaller scale.

Micronations are often quite small, in both their claimed territory and claimed populations — although there are some exceptions to this rule, with different micronations having different methods of citizenship. Micronations may also issue formal instruments such as postage stamps, coins, banknotes and passports, and bestow honours and titles of nobility." - *Micronation*, n.d., Wikipedia (accessed Dec. 7, 2017).

"In the present day, the following categories are generally accepted as being standard:

1. Social, economic, or political simulations.
2. Historical simulations.
3. Exercises in personal entertainment or self-aggrandisement.
4. Exercises in fantasy, creative fiction or artistic expression.
5. Vehicles for the promotion of an agenda.
6. Entities created for fraudulent purposes.
7. Historical anomalies and aspirant states.
8. Exercises in historical revisionism.
9. New-country projects.
10. Seasteading"

-*Micronation,* n.d., Micronations.Wikia (accessed Dec. 7, 2017)

The following is a compilation of sources of micronational law compiled by the people of the Cyanocitta Cristata Republic in order to create a centralized source of law and jurisprudence from the micronational community. Its contents are sourced from documents volunteered by their respective micronations and the public domain to be added into the Library of Micronational Law.[1]

3

The collection of the Library is woefully incomplete, limited by awareness, barriers of language, decisions by owners of documents not to submit, and the ephemeral nature and quickly-changing universe of micronations. This compilation is only more incomplete, including a more curated selection of documents. Not all micronations are represented here, and not all micronations produce documents which would find a home in this volume. However, it is the most complete collection of its kind, and it seeks to present an adequately representative look at the law of micronations around the world, both in how they bind and govern themselves and in how they interact with one another diplomatically.

The documents included are all from either extant micronations, those of significant notability which have become inactive, or from otherwise significant sources that warrant inclusion. They have been included here in as close to their original form as possible, with only the edits necessary for formatting and clarity as to their origin. Documents which are currently included by be removed from future versions if they do not fit any of these descriptions. This compilation will be under regular review, with a good-faith effort to include only the latest versions of the documents annually. With that in mind, the contents of this compilation should not be assumed up to date- it is to serve as a reference only.

Copies of these documents are available for free from the Library of Micronational Law at the location indicated in Footnote 1. Additionally, they are frequently accessible from the websites of their respective micronations. For more information about these documents or about including or removing a document, please contact the Curator.[2]

---

[1] The Library of Micronational Law is hosted here:
https://docs.google.com/spreadsheets/d/1t18_EQOGLn2WltrpzYPPss6AenGVh ⬩
MmR1nt-BDf2lQA/edit?usp=sharing

Many thanks to those who submitted documents for inclusion into the Library.

Inter-Micronational Treaties, Conventions, International Acts, and Protocols

The Alcatraz Environmental Treaty of 2015

Whereas we, the assembled Micronations of the 3rd International Conference on Micronations, have reached the conclusion that the large states of the world have been ineffective and their efforts have been lacking in intention and execution concerning efforts to improve the environment, preserve existing natural resources, and reduce carbon emissions to slow the change of the climate.

Therefore, we, the nations that are considered silly by the large nations, are entering into an agreement amongst ourselves to make a serious effort to preserve and protect our environments, and to ensure that we do everything within our power to reduce our communities' carbon emissions and slow/reverse the climatic change to ensure that our nations are not lost to the rising ocean levels.

We propose and agree to the following terms:

- We shall set an example for all nations and make a priority the preservation and protection of plants (flora) and animals (fauna) native to our respective communities through a combination of responsible/conservative use of natural resources, responsible agriculture, and water conservation. Special care will be taken to ensure the survival of local bee populations.

- We believe and agree that Antarctica is one of the few places on this planet to remain relatively untouched by humans and we strongly believe that it should remain a nature preserve only available to scientists for scientific research well beyond the expiration of the Antarctic Treaty in 2020.

- We shall set an example for all nations by creating highly localized sub-currencies that will promote the local production and consumption of goods and produce. Local production and consumption minimizes transport needs/costs and minimizes carbon emissions as a result of the reduced need for transport.

- We shall commit to researching and funding efforts to clean the human generated debris from the oceans and reduce the "garbage patches".

- We shall commit to structuring our financial systems in ways that strive to reduce poverty and elevate the standard of living for all of our peoples in an environmentally non-exploitative manner.

In addition, we demand, for every square foot of land or glacier lost to melting ice sheets and rising ocean levels, compensation from the large landed nations of one square meter of dry/non-threatened land so that we may relocate the climate refugees that will be created as a result of the rising waters.

Original Signatories:

The Royal Republic of Ladonia

The Free Republic of Alcatraz

The Republic of BennyLund

The Principality of Aigues-Mortes

The Grand Duchy of Flandrensis

Noseland

The Empire of Angyalistan

The Fomoire Institute

The Bundes Republik Neustadt.

Later Signatories*:

The Cyanocitta Cristata Republic

The Principality of Lorenzburg

*The list of later signatories is incomplete

Montevideo Convention on the Rights and Duties of States[3]

Montevideo Convention on the Rights and Duties of States

Done at: Montevideo

Date enacted: 1933-12-26

In force: 1934-12-26

Article 1

The state as a person of international law should possess the following qualifications:

a. a permanent population;

b. a defined territory;

c. government; and

---

[3] The Montevideo Convention and the principles it codifies are frequently touted by micronationalists as a legitimizing force for micronations, particularly Article 1, which defines statehood. Many micronations have declared themselves party to the convention, and others recognize themselves as bound to its principles as customary international law, as all states are. Others still, as an increasing number of international legal scholars do, reject the convention. The original signatories, preface, and reservations are omitted here.

d. capacity to enter into relations with the other states

Article 2

The federal state shall constitute a sole person in the eyes of international law.

Article 3

The political existence of the state is independent of recognition by the other states. Even before recognition the state has the right to defend its integrity and independence, to provide for its conservation and prosperity, and consequently to organize itself as it sees fit, to legislate upon its interests, administer its services, and to define the jurisdiction and competence of its courts. The exercise of these rights has no other limitation than the exercise of the rights of other states according to international law.

Article 4

States are juridically equal, enjoy the same rights, and have equal capacity in their exercise. The rights of each one do not depend upon the power which it possesses to assure its exercise, but upon the simple fact of its existence as a person under international law.

Article 5

The fundamental rights of states are not susceptible of being affected in any manner whatsoever.

Article 6

The recognition of a state merely signifies that the state which recognizes it accepts the personality of the other with all the rights and duties determined by international law. Recognition is unconditional and irrevocable.

Article 7

The recognition of a state may be express or tacit. The latter results from any act which implies the intention of recognizing the new state.

Article 8

No state has the right to intervene in the internal or external affairs of another.

Article 9

The jurisdiction of states within the limits of national territory applies to all the inhabitants. Nationals and foreigners are under the same protection of the law and the national authorities and the foreigners may not claim rights other or more extensive than those of the nationals.

Article 10

The primary interest of states is the conservation of peace. Differences of any nature which arise between them should be settled by recognized pacific methods.

Article 11

The contracting states definitely establish as the rule of their conduct the precise obligation not to recognize territorial acquisitions or special advantages which have been obtained by force whether this consists in the employment of arms, in threatening diplomatic representations, or in any other effective coercive measure. The territory of a state is inviolable and may not be the object of military occupation nor of other measures of force imposed by another state directly or indirectly or for any motive whatever even temporarily.

Article 12

The present Convention shall not affect obligations previously entered into by the High Contracting Parties by virtue of international agreements.

Article 13

The present Convention shall be ratified by the High Contracting Parties in conformity with their respective constitutional procedures. The Minister of Foreign Affairs of the Republic of Uruguay shall transmit authentic certified copies to the governments for the aforementioned purpose of ratification. The instrument of ratification shall be deposited in the archives of the Pan American Union in Washington, which shall notify the signatory governments of said deposit. Such notification shall be considered as an exchange of ratifications.

Article 14

The present Convention will enter into force between the High Contracting Parties in the order in which they deposit their respective ratifications.

Article 15

The present Convention shall remain in force indefinitely but may be denounced by means of one year's notice given to the Pan American Union, which shall transmit it to the other signatory governments. After the expiration of this period the Convention shall cease in its effects as regards the party which denounces but shall remain in effect for the remaining High Contracting Parties.

Article 16

The present Convention shall be open for the adherence and accession of the States which are not signatories. The corresponding instruments shall be deposited in the archives of the Pan American Union which shall communicate them to the other High Contracting Parties.

In witness whereof, the following Plenipotentiaries have signed this Convention in Spanish, English, Portuguese and French and hereunto affix their respective seals in the city of Montevideo, Republic of Uruguay, this 26th day of December, 1933.

The Laws of Micronations

Aerica[4]

Constitution[5]

Article 1: Government
Section 1: Executive and legislative power
Executive and legislative power is held by the Senate.

---

[4] More commonly known as the Aerican Empire, by all accounts.
[5] Original Source: http://www.aericanempire.com/con_0001.html

Section 2: The Senate

The Senate is the high government of the Aerican Empire, above and in some cases overriding the constitutions of individual colonies.

Clause 1: Senators are to be elected by colonies which they represent.

Clause 2: No colonies may have more than 2 members in the Senate.

Clause 3: Individuals shall not be barred from the Senate for reasons of age or creed, but all Senators must be elected knowingly by their constituents.

Clause 4: The Senate sits for a four year term. At the end of these four years, all Senate seats must be vacated, and new representatives elected in each colony. Senators who assumed their seats partway through this four year term must vacate their seats at the same time as all other Senators.

Clause 5: An election may be called before the end of a four year term by either the Emperor or the President of the Senate, at a time agreed upon by both parties, with three months notice. An election may be called with only one week's notice by the President to fill the empty seats of a colony.

Clause 6: If a Senator transmits to the Emperor or Senate his written declaration that he or she is unable to discharge the powers and duties of his or her office, and until he or she transmits a written declaration to the contrary, the responsibilities of that office shall be discharged by an Acting Senator, elected by the Senate.

Clause 7: A Senator may be removed from power by their constituency by a referendum thereof. Such a referendum will be scheduled by the Emperor upon the presentation to the Senate of a petition requesting a given Senator's removal, signed by twenty citizens within the constituency of the said Senator, or one sixth of the constituency's population, whichever is lesser. Upon the removal of a Senator from power, the President will, in consultation with the Emperor, schedule an election in the affected colony as soon as is practicable to elect a replacement Senator, as allowed by Article 1, Section 2, Clause 5.

Clause 8: No member of of the Senate shall hold a position in the government of another micronation.

Clause 9: One Senator shall be elected by the Senate to act as President of the Senate. This member shall moderate discussion and manage activity and voting.

Clause 10: The Emperor shall act as Vice-President of the Senate, fulfilling the duties of the President when there is no President or the President cannot fulfill his or her duties.

Section 3: The President
The President shall act as the moderator of the Senate.
Clause 1: The President will be a Senator. At the start of each four year term, the Senate will elect one member to act as President in addition to retaining their elected seat.
Clause 2: At the end of the Senate's four year term, the President shall vacate this position. The departing President may be re-elected by the Senate if he or she retains a Senate seat.
Clause 3: The duties of the President shall be to log all motions, to moderate all discussions within the Senate, and to promptly bring all motions to vote.

Section 4: The Secretary
The Secretary's duty shall be to maintain an accurate record of issues before the Senate, ensure that all issues are acted upon in order, and facilitate the Senate proceeding in a timely manner.
Clause 1: The President may appoint a Secretary from amongst the Senators.
Clause 2: It is the duty of the Secretary to take note of all proposals before the Senate and to help the President track which motions require attention.
Clause 3: The Secretary shall furthermore be responsible for tracking when discussions or voting periods have elapsed and bringing such lateness to the attention of the President and Senate.

Section 5: The Emperor
The Emperor will be the chief of state of the Aerican Empire.
Clause 1: The Emperor shall be chosen from amongst the Senate by majority vote of all Senators. When a Senator is proclaimed Emperor, he or she ceases to represent a colony, and their seat becomes vacant. The Emperor is considered to represent the whole of the Empire and receives one vote.
Clause 2: The Emperor may be selected from outside the Senate if two thirds (rounded down) plus one of all Senators vote in favour of this.
Clause 3: The position of Emperor will be held until death, abdication, or impeachment.
Clause 4: The powers of the Emperor shall be as follows:
1) In cases of deadlock, the Emperor may cast a second vote
2) In cases of war, the Emperor may supersede any military action
3) In cases of diplomacy, the Emperor may override the judgment of a

Minister

4) The Emperor shall have the sole power to appoint Ministers

Clause 5: The Emperor may be impeached by the Senate if there is a greater than 75% majority in favor.

Clause 6: To be elected emperor, a candidate must have been a citizen for no less than five years without interruption. This clause shall not come into effect in the event that no citizens meet this criterion at the time of a vacancy for the position of emperor. The outgoing emperor may name a chosen successor as a candidate for election who does not meet this qualification.

Section 6: Senatorial Conduct

Senators deemed by a two thirds (rounded down) plus one of the Senate to be acting in an improper manner shall lose their seat. Improper behaviour shall be defined as publically-made and recorded comments of a racist, sexist, or hateful nature which elicits complaints from no fewer than ten citizens made to their Senators or commission of and conviction for a criminal offense.

Section 7: Order of Action

Clause 1: The president of the Senate will present all motions for voting in the order in which they are proposed.

Clause 2: Motions deemed by the Senate to be urgent and motions relating to war, disaster, or diplomacy shall take precedence.

Section 8: Senatorial Powers

The powers of the Senate shall be as follows:

Clause 1: The Senate will have the power to: Coin money, control the military, control disaster relief, control intercolonial law, regulate intercolonial travel, control civilian ownership of armed vehicles and weapons, and set or abolish taxes.

Clause 2: The Senate will assume new powers as the need arises.

Section 9: The Ministries

The ministries shall be offices maintained by citizens appointed by the Emperor, which will fulfill standard government duties on behalf of the Emperor and Senate.

Clause 1: A minister shall be appointed by the Emperor for each ministry. This minister will have full control of the ministry, and is answerable to the Emperor and Senate.

Clause 2: The following ministries will exist:
Diplomacy and Foreign Affairs
Trade and Economics
Public Relations
Military Affairs
Information
Silly Things
Intergalactic Development
Clause 3: The Emperor may form or dissolve ministries and may choose to leave a ministry vacant if it is deemed temporarily unnecessary or no qualified candidates are available.

Article 2: Corollary Powers

Section 1: Religion
Each colony has the right to regulate the establishment of churches as it sees fit. No more than 3 members of a high rank of a given faith may sit in the Senate.
Clause 1: Any preacher, priest, rabbi (ad infinitum) must hold a Preacher's License to preach outside of their respective places of worship. No individual shall have the right to force their religious teachings upon an individual who is not a member of their congregation.

Section 2: Judicial Power
Each colony has the right to establish codes of law and justice.
Clause 1: Legal and judicial cases shall appear before the Supreme Court of the Empire.
Clause 2: The Supreme Court shall consist of members selected by the population of the Empire as a whole. The number of judges to sit on this court shall be no less than five, and as large as the population wishes to make it.

Article 3: Rights and Freedoms

Section 1: Rights
Clause 1: Citizens will have the rights to: Health care if not given by the respective government, funding for education if not given by the respective government, and funding for science if not given by the respective government. All citizens have the right to freedom of speech, the right to gather in groups, the right to non-violent protest, the right to political satire, and all basic rights and freedoms recognized by the United Nations.

14

Clause 2: No law shall have retroactive effect to the detriment of any person. No person shall be found in violation of any law of the Empire for an act committed before the ratification of such law, nor shall any penalty be imposed for an offense greater than the penalty prescribed by law at the time the offense was committed. Should any law be amended to provide for a lesser penalty for a given offense, the lighter penalty shall be applied to those previously or subsequently found in violation of the law; or if a law is amended so that a given act does not constitute an offense, no person shall be found in violation of the law for an act committed which no longer constitutes an offense.

Section 2: Requirements to Remain a Citizen
Citizens will be required to: be registered as a citizen of a registered world in the Empire, acknowledge the Senate and its power, and follow the dictates of their respective government unless otherwise dictated by the Senate.

Section 3: Equality
All citizens are equal. No race, religion, gender, society, political group, economic group, or social group shall be treated better than another.

Article 4: New Law and Amendments to the Constitution
A new law under consideration must be submitted to the Senate, where it will be voted upon.
Section 1: Laws
Clause 1: Each Senator has one vote. In cases where there is no Senatorial representation, or an area has only one Senator, empty seats are counted as abstentions. In the event of a tie, the Emperor may cast a second vote to break it.
Clause 2: For Senate votes, "majority" shall be considered to be a plurality, as defined as "an excess of votes over those cast for an opposing candidate." If the number of votes cast in favour of a motion exceeds the number cast in opposition, the motion will be considered to have passed by majority vote. A Senator who abstains in a vote is not counted towards the number who voted.
Clause 3: Any Senator may sponsor a motion. A second Senator must second this motion before it is considered for voting. If the Senate is not occupied with other business, yhe president of the Senate will call a vote on the motion within one month of seconding. If the Senate is occupied by other voting, the President may initiate a new vote or may delay

voting on new motions until current votes are completed. All votes must last for a minimum of one week and a maximum of one month and may be concluded early if all Senators have cast their vote.

Clause 4: The People may veto a law by petitioning the Senate. A petition of no less than one half the total population of the Empire (rounded down) must be presented to the Senate to veto a motion which affects multiple colonies, and a petition of no less than one half the total population of a colony (rounded down) must be presented to the Senate to veto a motion affecting only a single colony.

Clause 5: Any Senator who fails to vote during the assigned time shall be counted as an abstention.

Clause 6: A Senator may request that an upcoming or ongoing voting period be delayed or extended for up to fourteen days, not including weekends and Public Holidays, for any reason. A Senator may request this delay once for a given motion, and after the stated time is up, the Senator must vote or abstain.

Section 2: Amendments to the Constitution
Amendments to the Constitution shall be proposed to the Senate via the same procedure as new laws. The Senate shall have no less than forty-eight hours in which to decide if an amendment constitutes a major change to the constitution or a minor one.

Clause 1: If an amendment is deemed to be a minor change, the proposal is announced to the populace at large. The population shall have a minimum of 48 hours and a maximum of seven days in which to comment or object. If five non-Senator citizens or five percent of the population (whichever is more) object within that time, the amendment cannot be put forward for voting by the Senate. The amendment shall require a two-thirds majority in the Senate to be adopted.

Clause 2: If one-third of all Senators vote that an amendment is a major change, the proposal shall be announced to the populace at large and the populace shall have a period of no less than two weeks and no more than one month to comment or object. During and after this time, the Senate shall be free to attempt to address any such comments or objections and resubmit the proposal to the populace for no less than one additional week. At the end of this week, a referendum shall be held during which all citizens may vote to adopt or not adopt the amendment, and a plurality (as defined in Article 4, Section 1, Clause 2) shall be required for the amendment to be adopted.

Code of Law[6]

The Murphy Act

IN light of the future being for the most part unknown,
IN light of the fact that no person or persons can predict the needs that a government will have to fill,
IN light of the fact that whatever can go wrong, will go wrong,
The Aerican Senate does hereby put forth this law:
That as the need arises, due to changing structure, science, economy, or circumstance, that the Senate will assume power as is needed that it may best fulfill the needs of its people.

This document is set forth as law, by the Emperor of the Aerican Empire, by the Senate of the Aerican Empire, in accordance with all laws and statues put forth by said Empire.

The Diplomatic Policy

Full diplomatic relations:

As there are many micronational bodies existing at any time, with more being created as time passes, it is vital that a strong system of recognition or refusal be established by any nation. In light of this, the Aerican Empire hereby endorses these rules regarding its diplomatic contacts.

Any nation may be allowed to approach the Empire, and to make its case before the Empire. All nations shall receive a fair hearing by Imperial officials. To be fully recognized, nations must meet the following criteria:

- That the nation has a documented existence of at least 6 months
- That the nation holds no laws of a racist or hateful nature

---

[6] Original Source: http://www.aericanempire.com/law.html

- That the nation is not, at the time of application, actively in conflict with another ally of the Empire
- That, in reviewing the information provided by the nation, nothing is found which causes concern within the government

The following list is a compilation of the conditions upon which a nation may be rejected:

- Communicating entirely in capital letters
- Claiming as citizens all people living in their territory regardless of whether the citizens know the nation exists
- Claiming a false history

Conditional Diplomatic Relations:

Nations which meet all criteria above except for achieving six months of activity will be granted Conditional Recognition. This is exactly the same as full recognition save that in case of priority, the Conditionally Recognized nation will be given lower priority.

At the end of six months after independence, the nation may request that the Empire upgrade relations to full diplomatic relations. If the nation still meets all above criteria, full recognition will be granted.

Review of applicants:

The review of a nation will be carried out by careful study of all information presented by their nation, as well as a study of their web-site. Should an applicant nation be judged for some reason as being unsuitable for recognition, they will be approached and given a chance to make their case in their own defense.

Aerica will not discriminate by government, economic policy, religion or any other factor as long as that nation holds basic human rights.

Conflicts between the criteria and recognized nations:
If a nation is listed as recognized by the Empire but either does not fulfill the requirements of recognition, or violates the conditions upon which recognition will immediately be denied, then the likely answer is that

they were accepted before the clause in question was accepted as part of the diplomatic policy. New additions to the policy are not made retroactive, and only apply to nations who apply for recognition after the law is passed.

The War Act

As hate and fear are basic components in the human psyche,
As in the history of Humankind, there has been war almost incessantly,
As combat must be prepared for if a nation is to survive,
Then Aerica hereby establishes these laws as the War Act:
It is the goal of the Aerican Empire to avoid conflict. War can and must be avoided, if possible.
In the event of an ally of the Empire being pulled into war, Aerica shall offer to be a neutral arbitrator in this conflict.
Aerica shall investigate all conflicts to the best of its abilities, and not take sides until the situation has been judged.
In the event of Aerica being forced to enter into a war, it shall fight defensively if possible, to defend its land.
Under Wartime Conditions, Martial law is enforced on any area within the conflict, and the Emperor takes direct control with the help of the military.
Any other nation beginning a war with an ally of Aerica will be treated as a potential threat.
Aerica will not begin a conflict with another nation. It will only end the conflict.

This document is set forth as law, by the Emperor of the Aerican Empire, by the Senate of the Aerican Empire, in accordance with all laws and statues put forth by said Empire.

The Monarchy Act

Section 1 Powers
The Royal Family of Aerica shall have no official powers, and shall be considered a "figurehead Family"

Section 2 Members
Subsection 1
The Royal Family shall consist of;
1 King, 1 Queen, 1 Prince, 1 Princess and 1 Court Wizard.
Subsection 2
The Royal Family has the right to appoint a Royal Court of their choosing.

Section 3 Terms of Office
Subsection 1
The members of the Royal Family are to be elected by the people of Aerica.
Subsection 2
The members of the Royal Family are elected for life.

Section 4 Abdication/removal of member
Subsection 1 Abdication
Any Member of the Royal Family may abdicate their throne by simply transmitting a letter or e-mail to the Aerican mailing list at Yahoo Groups or succeeding service, stating that they no longer will or are able to hold their position.
Subsection 2 Forcible Removal from Office
The Senate holds the right to remove a member of the Royal Family from office for the following reasons;
Treason, Being Culled, Loss of Citizenship, Acting in a manner detrimental to the good of the Nation or conviction of High Crimes.
The Senate will follow the same procedures as for removal of the Emperor.

Section 5 Prohibited Acts
The members of the Royal Family are prohibited from the following;
1 Holding office in another micronation
2 Being a member of a Royal Family of any other micronation.
3 Using their office for personal gain.
4 Misrepresenting themselves as having official powers in Aerica.

The Hillary Clinton Act

Adopted into law: 10/18/01

A citizen of any colony may run for a senate seat in another colony provided that if said citizen wins, he or she must move to the colony he or she represents.

Y-BON Protocol[7]

The Y-BON Protocol

In response to an email declaring micronational war, the respondent shall compose a brief and polite reply according to the following steps:

1) Thank the individual for their interest in the Aerican Empire and express happiness that our nation has inspired their imagination

2) Inform the recipient that the Aerican Empire considers micronational war to be an impossibility. Optionally, the respondent may elaborate that it is "an impossibility at best and (insert derogatory adjective here, such as idiocy, inanity, foolishness...) at worst."

3) Inform the recipient that, as per the Y-BON protocol of 2015, you will be blocking their email after sending this reply, and so you will regretfully not receive any further messages they choose to send.

4) Advise them that you will be forwarding their recent communications, as well as their name and IP address, to the relevant local law enforcement (ex: the United States IC3, the Australian ACORN, the Canadian RCMP, etc.). It is up to the individual's discretion to decide whether a case actually merits reporting since generally such declarations

---

[7] This protocol for dealing with pointless declarations of micronational war has been adapted and adopted by certain other micronations to deter juvenile activity.

of war do not escalate to the level of threats that an agency will take seriously, but as most individuals declaring "war" are unaware that such enforcement agencies even exist, the threat should be enough to make them think twice about saying Bloody Stupid Things.

5) Thank them again and wish them well in future diplomatic initiatives.

Remember always that when enacting the Y-BON Protocol, remain unfailingly polite and courteous, as nothing else will infuriate the recipient quite as much.

Rather than compose new letters, if they wish, individuals with access to the foreign affairs communication archive (AEEEdfm06) are invited to take a previously-composed letter, remembering of course to change the sender's and recipient's names as appropriate.

Arkonia
Treaty of Mutual Cooperation with Ethia

On this day, February Twenty-Seventh, Two Thousand and Seventeen, the Federal Kingdom of Arkonia and the Ethian Republic. Each country will support the others with ideas and other non-material items.

Article 1: Embassies

Arkonia and Ethia will build embassies in each other's countries. These embassies will contain flags of each country.

Article 2: Trading

Arkonia and Ethia will trade ideas and other non-material goods. The nations will not trade due to the distance between the two nations.

California Valley
Constitution

THE CONSTITUTION OF THE CALIFORNIA VALLEY DEMOCRATIC PEOPLE'S REPUBLIC

A.   We, the free people of the California Valley Democratic People's Republic, with self determination, in order to form a free state, and to achieve within the confines of free statehood, an independent nation, dedicated to freedom of its people, and to create a free, sustainable, healthy state dedicated to the sustainable future of planet earth and to achieve other defined goals of free statehood, do hereby establish this Constitution as the founding document of the California Valley Democratic People's Republic (C.V.R) on the date of MAY THE 1ST, YEAR 2018

I.   THE PEOPLE'S GOVERNMENT

1A. The California Valley Democratic People's Republic based on the idea of citizen representation will always maintain a transparent and open system of government. Although this system will adapt overtime, it will always remain a free and unrestricted democracy, ran by and always serving the best interest of the people

1B. At the time of the founding of the C.V.R, the executive branch will be the power of the PRESIDENT OF THE CALIFORNIA VALLEY PEOPLE'S REPUBLIC. At the date of founding the President shall be Devin Negrete. This first Term will have no limit, and the current President, Devin Negrete, Shall hold office till Death, Self removal or impeachment.

1B2. Upon removal of Devin Negrete from office of the President upon Death, Self Removal or impeachment, The President Shall be Decided by an Election, That will take Place on the 1st of June the following year of removal from office.

1B3. In the event that citizens find the standing president to be unfit to hold office, there right to impeach shall never be removed. The impeachment and removal process for the President at the date of founding, Devin Negrete, shall be a 100 percent popular vote in favor of impeachment, counted against all those who voted. Upon the term of the next standing president immediately following the President at the date of founding Devin Negrete, The impeachment process will be changed to a popular vote of 51% or more majority in favor of impeachment

1B3. In the event of JUDICIAL IMPEACHMENT, in which the President has been accused of breaking one or more felony laws, then a majority vote of the senate will take place for impeachment. An impeachment will require a majority vote of 51% in favor, allowing for 2 abstentions. In the event of a tie, the vote will be determined by citizen election.

1B4. All Military and National Defense Power will in the power of the executive branch. The decision to declare war must be voted on by the senate, winning with a 75% majority vote. It is possible for the senate to mediate the vote to a citizen vote in which 60% majority vote in favor will win

1B5. The president can propose any law, without requiring a vote and pass it into law. The senate can override any executive law with a 75% percent majority vote in favor against

1B6. The president will be responsible for appointing and maintaining the executive cabinet of directors

1B7. The executive branch will have power over the Intelligence Department

1C. The People's Assembly is the senate of the C.V.R consisting of voted representatives from each district. Each District will elect two representatives as well as two voting members to the people's assembly through popular vote. An election will occur every TWO YEARS on the First of JUNE. The People's will have the responsibility of drafting the laws that govern our free nation and the elected representatives will be direct representatives of the people with great pride and duty to do everything they can to strengthen their community and district

1C2. The SENATE ASSEMBLY LEADER will be the voted leader of the each assembly meetings, voting will take place at the commencement of each years Senate year, which begins on JUNE THE FIRST. The vote will be a majority vote and only one senator from each district can choose to be the electorate for the senate assembly leader position.

1C3. Any member of the people's assembly can purpose a legislative bill to enter into proposal during the current assembly or during the following days assembly. If a senator proposes a bill, and then fails to enact a call for a vote, that bill verbatim may not be purposed again for 120 days. The process of proposal will be Initial Proposal, Floor Debate, and Vote

1C3B. Initial proposal will be the a 8 minute proposal for said bill by the sponsoring senator. Any opposition following the proposal is open but limited to one speaker for 2 minutes

1C3C. Floor Debate shall consist of two ten minute arguments by ONE SENATOR for each position, for or against the bill. IF THERE IS NO OPPOSITION TO SAID BILL, A MOTION CAN BE CALLED TO A QUICK VOTE, IN WHICH THE MOVE WILL BE DIRECTLY TO A VOTE AND FLOOR DEBATE

25

WILL BE SKIPPED. THE QUICK VOTE MUST TAKE PLACE DURING THE SAME ASSEMBLY DAY

        1C3C. If a quick vote fails to pass bill, it may enter back into floor debate. A bill can only enter quick vote once during its assembly cycle

        1C3D. Voting will be a majority 51% win vote by senators. The Assembly Leader may not vote on a bill unless there is a tie

    1D. The people's court will consist of THE DISTRICT COURTS and the PEOPLES FEDERAL COURT. 4 elected judges also consisting of one senator will be elected very 8 years by citizen popular vote. Each district will have 1 judge voted by citizen popular vote every 4 years.

II . The Monarchy will be established at the founding of the People's Republic. Antonio Negrete, of the House of Guerro will be acting KING OF THE CALIFORNIA CENTRAL VALLEY untill death or self removal. The king will be a figurehead placement only, acting as a symbol of our nation. The standing king will have no executive, legislative or judicial power.

    2E2. The king and royal family are immune from any judicial action. Election to a government position denotes any immunity till arrest while holding office

    2E3. Upon removal, the royal hier will be appointed as the KING.

III. Changes or Amendments to the Constitution will take place in the same manner in which laws are proposed. The executive and legislative branches can both purpose changes

26

IV. Two types of Citizenship will exist. Residential Citizenship or General Citizenship will be available to any citizen with currently permanent residing residence in the C.V.R or someone who has resided into the C.V.R for more than 1 year. After 1 year of residency, permanent citizenship is attainted. The second type of Citizenship Available is Intermittent Citizenship which is limited Citizenship granted to people living permanently or temporarily outside of the C.V.R or currently in a residential entry waiting program.

4B. Only citizens currently residing inside of the C.V.R will be subject to taxation

4C. Citizens with PRE-PERMANENT RESIDENTIAL CITIZENSHIP who reside within the CVR for less than a year, will maintain residential citizenship for up to ONE YEAR while residing outside of the C.V.R. After one year of residing outside of the C.V.R the citizenship status will be downgraded to intermittent

CONSTITUTION END

RATIFIED
MAY THE FIRST, YEAR 2018

Ratified by the FIRSTS PEOPLE'S ASSEMBLY

Cyanocitta

Code

The Code of the Cyanocitta Isopod's Republic

§1- This Code shall be the controlling Code of the Cyanocitta Isopod's Republic, effective across all it's territories. (30/8/2017)

§2- The Glorious Leader shall be the source of all Executive, Legislative, and Judicial power. (30/8/2017)

§3- When a vote is authorized, it shall take place via the placement of tubes labeled with the various positions on the matter, to be placed for not less than 24 hours and equipped with sufficient food and water. Each citizen present in a tube at the closing of the polls shall constitute a vote for that position labeled on the given container. (30/8/2017)

§4- Armadillidium vulgare within the Republic are citizens. (30/8/2017)

§5- The Kingdon stands for sustainability, equity, and fairness. Half of its income shall go to these ends across the planet. (30/8/2017)

§6- Except in the name of public safety, no mining of minerals or metals shall take place in the Republic. (30/8/2017)

§7- All farming done within the Republic must be done per Organic standards set by the USDA. (30/8/2017)

§8- Use of motor vehicles for personal or industrial purposes shall be unlawful within the Republic. (30/8/2017)

§9- No female with fertilized eggs or brood shall be subjected to testing unless that testing is related to her reproduction. (30/8/2017)

§10- No Isopod may freely depart the Republic. (30/8/2017)

§11- Only Isopods four millimeters or longer, head to rear carapace, shall be eligible to vote. (30/8/2017)

§12- No private ownership of real property shall be permitted. (31/8/2017)

§13- Except in cases of pregnant females or in cases of dangerously imbalanced sex ratios, there shall be no discrimination on the basis of sex between citizens. (6/9/2017)

§14- Energy used in the Republic must be generated in such a way as to be carbon neutral, or not at all. (10/9/2017)

§15- Spiders may remain within the Republic so long as no consumption of Isopods occurs, or until definite risk of such consumption appears imminent. (20/9/2017)

§16- The Republic shall be bound by the terms of the Alcatraz Environmental Treaty of 2015. (29/9/2017)

§17- No ants shall come within one foot of the Republic's territory. If ants are discovered in violation, all efforts shall be authorized to purge them from such proximity. (15/10/2017)

§18- No one shall discriminate against an Isopod on the basis of differing species. The Republic shall not discriminate against an Isopod on the basis of differing species without a compelling state interest for doing so. (22/10/2017)

§19- State financial productivity from acts of Isopod citizens shall only be used to their benefit or for their purposes. (7/2/2017)

§20- It shall be unlawful for an Isopod to climb higher than three inches from a solid surface along the walls of a tank. (7/3/2017)

§21- The Ministry of Human Affairs is hereby created and tasked with promulgating rules relating to humans and the Republic. (9/5/2018)

Francisville[8]

Constitution

Constitution of the Federal Republic of Francsisville

Title 1 – General Provisions

Article 1: Name

The name of the state is the Federal Republic of Francisville. Its shortened form is Francisville.

Article 2: Democratic State and Rule of Law

(I) Francisville is a free, fair, and open democratic state, based on the rule of the law, the sovereignty of the people, and the protection of individual rights.

(II) The organs of state are established for the protection of the sovereignty and security of the nation, and the protection of human rights and dignity.

Article 3: Secular State

Francisville is a secular state. The state affords no favours to any religious group.

Article 4: Cantons

(I) The state is a federation composed of the cantons of Wasserbrueck, New

Scireland, North Llabdey, and Rudno.

---

[8] Franscisville was fully dissolved in 2014, but is retained in this edition of this compilation as an exemplar of legal texts in a federal micronational system.

(II) The cantons are sovereign insofar as their sovereignty is not limited by the Federal constitution and federal law. They exercise their powers accordingly.

Article 5: Sovereignty

(I) National sovereignty rests with the people, and is exercised through the constitution.

(II) All power emanates from the people. The state is fully answerable to the public and holds the burden of proof for its authority.

(III) The state is subject to the constitution. The Federal constitution and Federal law apply throughout the nation.

Article 6: Territory and Land Claims

(I) The right to make territorial claims rests with the cantons.

(II) The process of claiming territory, the settling of boundary disputes, and the limits of territorial waters shall be regulated by federal law.

(III) Territorial claims are restricted to land on planet earth.

Article 7: National Symbols

(I) The national flag of Francisville consists of three equal horizontal bands of dark red followed by white followed by dark blue. The centre of the white band contains black scales of justice.

(II) Other national symbols may be adopted by the Federal Council.

(III) The demonym of Francisville is Francillian.

Article 8: Languages

(I) All federal legislation shall be drafted in English.

(II) The cantons regulate their own official languages with respect for linguistic minorities.

(III) All public authorities shall ensure that public information is comprehensible to all citizens.

Title 2 – Fundamental Rights and Freedoms

Chapter 1 - General provisions

Article 9: The Person

A person shall describe any living human being regardless of citizenship, residency, nationality, or physical and mental ability.

Article 10: Francillian Citizenship

(I) Federal law regulates Francillian citizenship

(II) A citizen is considered both a citizen of the Federation and a citizen of their canton.

(III) Citizenship can only be removed by the courts through due process of the law.

(IV) A Francillian Citizen may renounce their citizenship at any time by

addressing a signed document to the Federal Council.

Article 11: Citizens Domiciled Abroad

(I) The state shall grant all citizens living abroad equal rights and to those living

within Francisville, as laid down by this constitution.

(II) The state shall facilitate links between the Federation and citizens domiciled abroad.

(III) Status as a Francillian citizen does not protect a person from the law of any other country they enter or in which they hold citizenship.

Article 12: Universality

All rights laid down by the provisions this constitution shall be enjoyed universally and be upheld in all areas of the state.

Article 13: Equality

(I) All people are equal before the law.

(II) All people are born equal. Francisville has no class system, nobility, or similar system of social distinction or privilege.

(III) No person may be favoured or disadvantaged because of sex, gender, sexual orientation, parentage, ancestry, ethnicity, race, nationality, place of origin, creed, language, religion, spirituality, faith, political convictions, conscience, education, economic situation, social situation, education, or physical or mental capabilities.

Article 14: Inviolability

Fundamental human rights are the utmost protection of human life, dignity, and freedom. The state may not under any circumstances contravene these Fundamental rights except by the provisions of this constitution.

Article 15: Additional Human Rights

Additional rights may be adopted and regulated by law.

Article 16: Liability of the State

The state and all its organs are held directly responsible for any actions they undertake which violate fundamental human rights or the duties of another organ of state.

Article 17: Right to Protest

(I) Every person has the right to protest to the state if the rights granted to them by this constitution are violated.

(II) The state has the responsibility to report and investigate violations of rights and freedoms by due process of the law.

Article 18: Right to Resist

Every person has the right to resist any action or power which violates their rights, and may act with aggression as a direct response to aggression forced upon them if no other remedy be possible.

Chapter 2- Rights and Freedoms

Section 1- Fundamental Human Rights

Article 19: Right to Life

(I) All persons have the right to life. No person may be forcibly deprived of it.

(II) Capital punishment is prohibited in all circumstances.

Article 20: Human Dignity

(I) The physical and moral integrity of every person is safeguarded

(II) Every person has the right to respect and the protection of their personal dignity, image, and reputation.

(III) No person may be subjected to cruel, inhumane, unclean, or degrading punishment.

Article 21: Protection of Personal Privacy

(I) Every person has the right to the protection of the privacy of their personal life, home, and personal data.

(II) Privacy may only be infringed for the prevention of crime, and only by means and in cases laid down by the law.

Article 22: Right to Personal Liberty

(I) Individual liberty is inviolable. It may only be removed by the courts in accordance with the law as a criminal punishment, or for the protection of security by virtue of the law.

(II) Conscription is prohibited.

(III) Every person may act freely without violating the freedom of others, and whilst being in accordance with the law.

Article 23: Freedom of Religion and Conscience

(I) Freedom of religion, faith, spirituality, conscience and creed are inviolable.

(II) Public worship and ceremony are inviolable except for the prevention of criminal offences carried out whilst using this freedom.

(III) The freedom to join, establish, or administer religious institutions, organisations, and communities without persecution or interference is inviolable. The state may not dictate in the membership of such organisations nor in the appointment of religious hierarchy.

(IV) The right of any religious group to teach and use its own means of public information are protected.

(v) No person shall be discriminated against for their refusal to supply information about their religious convictions or practices.

Article 24: Freedom of Expression

(I) Every person has the right to express and develop their views and opinions by speech, writing, images, or any other free means without persecution or interference.

(II) Every person has the right to develop their individuality and personality by means of speech, writing, and images through artistic and intellectual means.

Article 25: Freedom of Assembly

(I) All people have the right to meet and assembly peacefully and without arms without prior authorization.

(II) The right to hold open air meetings on private property is inviolable.

(III) The right to hold open air meetings on public property may be restricted for public order, security, and public convenience in a manner laid down by the law.

Article 26: Freedom of Association

(I) All citizens have the right to form clubs, societies and similar organisations.

(II) No person may be forced to or prevented from joining any organisation or to remain in it. Membership regulations of organisations are set without the interference of the state.

(III) Clubs, organisations, and societies have the right to organize themselves without the interference of the state.

Article 27: Inviolability of the Home

(I) The Home is inviolable.

(II) Forced entry into and search of the home is only permitted for the protection of public security and prevention of crime for reasons and by manners laid down by the law, and if given prior authorization by an organ of state by the provisions of the law.

(III) Searches of the home must not be carried out in such a way that causes immediate public danger, damage to life, or damage to property out with the authorization of the search.

Article 28: Marriage and Procreation

(I) The regulation and recognition of marriage and divorce are controlled by federal law with regard for the principles of equality and self-determination.

(II) All adults have the right to procreate in private, and to have children.

Article 29: Protection of Children

(I) Parents have the right and duty to bring up and care for their children provided they are able to provide the child with suitable welfare.

(II) Parents may only be forcibly separated from their children if the children are endangered or neglected whilst in their care. This may only be carried out by order of the courts in accordance with the provisions of the law.

(III) Adoption and abortion are regulated by federal law.

(IV) Federal law regulates the age at which a child is considered personally and criminally responsible and the age of adulthood.

Article 30: Right to Education and Teaching

(I) The right to learn and the right to teach are safeguarded.

(II) Public education shall be non-denomination, and afford no privilege to any particular religious or political ideology.

Article 31: Freedom of Creativity and Art

Every person has the right to artistic expression and creation be it written, performing or visual.

Article 32: Freedom of Science and Research

(I) Every person has the right to carry out scientific research

(II) This right may only be restricted for the protection of public security by the provisions of the law.

Article 33: Freedom from Slavery

(I) No person may ever be kept or sold as a slave.

(II) The attempt to establish a slave trade shall be a criminal offence.

Article 34: Integrity of Personal Communication

(I) The privacy and integrity of personal correspondence is safeguarded.

(II) Public authorities may only infringe this right in cases and by means laid down by the law for the prevention of crime.

Article 35: Freedom of Press and Media

(I) Freedom of the press and media is safeguarded. No licence or qualification may be introduced as a requirement to operate free press

(II) Censorship is prohibited.

(IV) Restrictions may be introduced to prevent the distribution of adult material to children.

Article 36: Freedom of Movement

(I) Francillian citizens have the right to freely travel and settle within the country.

(II) The right to leave and return to national territory is secured to all citizens.

Article 37: Freedom of Language

The right of every person to communicate in the language of their choice is protected.

Article 38: Freedom of Information

(I) Every person has the right to receive, gather, and disseminate information by legal means without interference or persecution.

(II) Every person has the right to access public information without the need for any qualification.

(III) Every person has the right access to personal data about themselves held by the state, and to demand information concerning its use.

Article 39: Freedom from Extradition and Right of Asylum

(I) Francillian citizens may only be extradited to another country with their consent.

(II) No person may be extradited to a country where they face persecution, cruel or inhumane treatment, or capital punishment.

(III) The Federation provides the right of asylum to protect aliens from persecution.

Article 40: Right to a Fair Trial and Lawful Judge

(I) Every person has the right to a fair, impartial trial carried out within reasonable time by due process of the law.

(II) Every person has the right to have their legal proceedings overseen by a lawful judge in good standing.

(III) No person may be unwillingly separated from the judge assigned to them by the courts.

Article 41: Fair and Legitimate Punishment

(I) No person may be subjected to any punishment that is not delivered through due process of the law.

(II) No person may be delivered a punishment that was not in force at the time when the crime was committed.

Article 42: Remand in Custody

(I) Every person is protected against arbitrary arrest, detention, and punishment.

(II) Remand in custody for more than forty-eight hours without charge is subject to judicial review.

(III) Remand in custody shall be considered exceptional in nature. The courts should favour alternative measures if appropriate.

(iv) The law shall impose a time limit on remand in custody

Article 43: Application of Criminal Law

(I) Every person is presumed to be innocent until proven to be otherwise through judicial procedure.

(II) Every person who is charged with a crime or has their freedoms restricted has the right to be informed properly of the charge brought against them and the reason for these restrictions promptly and in a language that they understand.

(III) No person shall be convicted for a crime that was not illegal at the time when it was committed.

(IV) No person shall be tried more than once for the same crime.

Article 44: Universal Access to the Courts

(I) Access to the courts is universal. Every person is guaranteed legal proceedings.

(II) Equal representation between parties is guaranteed in judicial proceedings. The law provides for legal aid if it is necessary in order for this right to be realised.

(III) Trials are public. The law may provide for exceptions for reasons of security and the protection of fundamental human rights.

Article 45: Habeas Corpus

(I) The right of Habeas Corpus is guaranteed as protection against unlawful arrest, detention, and punishment.

(II) The right of Habeas Corpus can be demanded by the concerned individual or by any citizen enjoying full political rights.

(II) A hearing as a result of such a demand shall be organised within fourteen days.

Article 46: Realisation of Fundamental Human Rights

(I) Fundamental human rights shall be realised in all areas of the state and legal system

(II) The state ensures that fundamental human rights are protected in private relations and enterprise.

Article 47: Restriction of Fundamental Human Rights

(I) Restrictions on fundamental human rights require a basis in federal law.

(II) Restrictions on fundamental human rights are permitted only if provided for by provisions of the article itself.

(III) Restrictions on fundamental human rights must conform to the principle of proportionality.

(IV) The general essence of any fundamental human right is inviolable.

Section 2- Political Rights

Article 48: Participation in Public Life

Every citizen has the right to participate in public life through the provisions of the constitution and the law.

Article 49: Right to Vote

(I) All citizens who have reached the age of fourteen have the right to vote and participate in the democratic process at all levels of the state.

(II) The cantons decide the democratic rights of residents without citizenship within the bounds of federal law.

(III) All ballots are secret.

(IV) No addition conditions for the right to vote may be imposed.

Article 50: Access to Public Office

(I) All citizens who have reached the age of fourteen and who have the right to vote are eligible for election at all levels of the state.

(II) No additional conditions for access to public office may be imposed expect to guarantee the seperation of powers.

Article 51: Political Parties and Organisations

(I) All citizens have the right to form political parties and organisations and operate them without interference from the state.

(II) All citizens have the right to join political parties and organisations under the principle of freedom of association.

Article 52: Exercise of Political Rights

(I) Political rights are exercised by citizens in their home canton.

(II) No person may exercise political rights in more than one canton.

(III) The Federation and the cantons make provisions to ensure the realisation of political rights.

Article 53: Restriction of Political Rights

(I) Restrictions on political rights require a basis in federal law.

(II) Restrictions on political rights are limited to the conditions of criminal punishment and mental incapacity.

(III) Restrictions on political rights must conform to the principle of proportionality and cause no damage to the realisation of fundamental human rights.

Section 3- Economic Rights and Social Aims

Article 54: Freedom to Work

(I) Every person has the right and the responsibility to work and the freedom to choose their occupation.

(II) The state aims to ensure the social protection of those who are not able to work and their dependents, be it due to disability or unavoidable personal responsibilities.

Article 55: Freedom to Unionise and Collective Bargaining

(I) All employers and employees have the right to unionise and form associations for the protection of their interests under the principle of freedom of association

(II) No person may be discriminated against in the workplace for their membership in any such organisation nor forced to pay fees to a union of which they are not a member.

(II) The state may aid collective bargaining within the scope of its powers.

Article 56: Rights of Workers

(I) All workers have the right to safe and healthy working conditions

(II) All workers are entitled to a limited working day and to reasonable working hours as set by law.

(III) All workers are entitles to rest and leisure, and to minimum paid holidays as set by law.

(IV) All workers have the right to adequate pay and to equal pay for equal work.

(V) The state aims to protect and aid workers in the workplace and during times of involuntary unemployment.

Article 57: Right to Private Property

(I) The right to own and to transfer private property is guaranteed.

(II) Expropriation of private property for public use requires a basis in law, and the payment of fair compensation.

Article 58: Private Enterprise and Economic Freedom

(I) Every person has the right to freely participate in private economic activity within the limits of the law.

(II) The right to industrial self-management and collective ownership is guaranteed.

(III) The law regulates private enterprise to prevent fraudulent activity and protect the interests of consumers.

Article 59: Limitations on Legal Personality

(I) Legal personality may only be granted to profit making entities if they remain under direct public control or conform to the principle of mutuality.

(II) The status of legal personality must not compromise or exceed the rights of natural persons.

Article 60: Right to Education

(I) Every person has the right to adequate, free, basic education based on the principle of freedom of opportunity, and suited to their needs and capacities.

(II) The state aims to provide equal access to education based on ability to all citizens throughout their lives.

Article 61: Right to Health

(I) Every person has the right to adequate protection of their health regardless of their economic situation, and has the social duty to protect it.

(II) Every person has the right to a safe and healthy working and living environment.

(III) Every person has the right to assistance during emergency if they are not able to provide it.

Article 62: Right to Adequate Dwelling

(I) Every person has the right to an adequately sized dwelling and the basic conveniences necessary to live a healthy and dignified life.

(II) The state aims to protect people from homelessness, and to ensure that housing is of a decent standard.

Article 63: Children and Young People

(I) Children and young people have the right to be protected from poverty and mistreatment.

(II) The state aims to ensure that abandoned and orphaned children are suitably cared for.

(III) The state aims to further the education and personal development of young people, and to encourage their involvement in society.

Article 64: Old Age

(I) Old people have the right to adequate living conditions, and aid for their specialised needs.

(II) The state aims to ensure economic security in old age, and to prevent the social marginalisation of the old.

Article 65: Family

(I) Parents have the right to protection and support in carrying out their duties.

(II) Parents have the right to adequately paid maternity leave, and to special dispensations in the workplace.

(III) The state recognises the importance of the social role of family units.

Article 66: State and Social Responsibility

(I) Economic rights and social aims do not eliminate individual social responsibility.

(II) No direct claim to state subsidies may be derived from social aims.

Title 3 – Federation, Cantons, and the People

Chapter 1- Cooperation between the Federation and the Cantons

Article 67: General Principles of Cooperation

(I) The Federation and the cantons work together, remain open with each other, and aid each other in their responsibilities.

(II) The Federation involves the cantons in federal decision making, and considers the interest of the cantons in its decisions.

(III) Disputes between the Federation and the cantons shall be resolved through peaceful negotiation.

Article 68: Allocation of Tasks

(I) The Federation fulfils the tasks allocated to it by the Federal Constitution and federal law.

(II) The Federation shall leave the cantons with sufficient tasks of their own, and provides financial assistance to the cantons for any responsibilities that it imposes on them.

(III) The principle of subsidiarity is upheld in the allocation of state responsibilities.

Article 69: Supremacy of Federal Law

Federal law takes supremacy over cantonal law. The cantons have the duty to implement it in accordance with the Federal Constitution.

Article 70: Intercantonal Cooperation

(I) Cantons may establish Intercantonal agreements and institutions within the boundaries of federal law.

(II) The Federation may facilitate intercantonal negotiation within the scope of its powers.

Article 71: Local Communities

(I) The cantons decide the authority and autonomy of local communities and administrative divisions.

(II) The Federation may regulate in order to promote and protect the autonomy of local communities.

Chapter 2- Cantons and the People

Article 72: Constitutional Order of Cantons

(I) Every canton adopts a constitutional order based on the principles of a free, republican, secular state governed by the rule of law as espoused by the Federal Constitution.

(II) Cantonal constitutions must be capable of being revised should the majority of eligible voters demand it.

(III) Cantons establish a non-partisan direct or representative democratic system and recognise the sovereignty of the people.

(III) Cantonal constitutions guarantee membership in the Federation, the supremacy of federal law, and the protection of Fundamental Rights and Freedoms.

Article 73: Federal Protection of Constitutional Order

(I) The Federation has the duty to protect the constitutional order of the cantons.

(II) The Federation may intervene when cantonal constitutional order is threatened.

Article 74: Federal Coercion

The Federation may take action against cantons which fail to implement or comply with the Federal Constitution or federal law by means of federal coercion.

Article 75: Cantonal Structure

(I) The restructuring of cantons including the merging of, and the secession and formation of new cantons requires the majority approval of the public in all regions concerned, and the approval of the Federal Council.

(II) The admission of new cantons is subject to the process of constitutional alteration. The approval of the majority of citizens in the concerned region is required.

Chapter 3- Powers

Section 1- Foreign relations, defence and law enforcement

Article 76: International Relations

(I) International relations are the responsibility of the Federation.

(II) The Federation is conscious of the interests and responsibilities of the cantons in exercising foreign policy.

Article 77: Principles of Foreign Policy

(I) In its foreign policy, the Federation promotes:

a) the protection of national sovereignty and the right to self-determination

b) the preservation of human rights and the promotion of democratic values

c) the alleviation of poverty, suffering, and injustice.

d) peaceful existence and cooperation between nations

e) the protection of natural resources and concern for environmental

issues

(II) The Federation values honesty and integrity in its international agreements.

Article 78: Neutrality

(I) Francisville is a neutral country.

(II) Acts which endanger the peaceful coexistence between nations or initiate a state of war or aggression are prohibited.

Article 79: International Organisations

(I) Assent to an international organisation requires the enactment of a federal statute.

(II) Membership in international organisations which entail military alliances or the supremacy of international institutions over the federal authorities is prohibited.

Article 80: Foreign Relations of Cantons

(I) The cantons may exercise foreign relations within the scope of their powers.

(II) Cantonal foreign relations are subject to the same regulations as federal foreign relations

(III) The cantons must inform the Federation when foreign agreements are signed.

Article 81: Humanitarian Aid

A minimum of three per cent of the federal budget shall be dedicated to humanitarian aid

Article 82: Militia

(I) Standing armies are prohibited.

(II) The Federation may establish a militia for national security and civil defence.

(III) The Federation regulates the use of any militia and its organisation shall conform to the principle of subsidiarity.

Article 83: Civil Defence

(I) The Federation adopts regulations on civil defence in emergencies and catastrophes.

(II) The Federation may obligate the cantons to provide civil defence in such circumstances.

Article 84: Arms and Weaponry

(I) The Federation adopts regulations on the ownership, use, and production of arms and weaponry.

(II) The importation, production, and use of military material require a basis in federal law.

(II) The use of nuclear weaponry is prohibited and it is forbidden from Francillian territory.

Article 85: Law Enforcement

(I) Law enforcement is the responsibility of the cantons.

(II) The Federation aids criminal investigation and cooperation between cantonal law enforcement agencies.

Section 2- Education and Research

Article 86: Education System

(I) The school system is the responsibility of the cantons.

(II) The cantons aim to provide free, basic, primary education for all children.

(III) The cantons aim to provide accessible, free, and varied secondary education.

(III) The aims of the education system shall be:

a) to ensure literacy

b) to provide for the special needs of all children

c) to encourage the personal development and skills of all children

d) to encourage academic and creative development

e) to promote equality, social participation, and individual responsibility

(IV) The Federation introduces regulations to ensure the harmonisation of cantonal education systems.

Article 87: Higher Education

(I) Higher education is the joint responsibility of the Federation and the cantons.

(II) The Federation establishes a federal, public university.

(III) The Federation may support cantonal universities and establish other higher education institutions.

(IV) The Federation encourages a high standard of professional and vocational education.

(V) In the advancement of higher education, the Federation may cooperate with foreign institutions of higher education within the scope of its powers.

Article 88: Research

(I) The Federation supports academic research and technological development.

(II) The Federation may establish its own research institutions.

Article 89: Culture and Sport

(I) The education system considers the importance of the roles of culture and sport.

(II) The Federation may encourage measures to support art and music, and may establish higher education institutions in these domains.

(III) The education system is conscious of cultural and linguistic diversity.

Section 3- Environment and Infrastructure

Article 90: Environmental Protection

(I) The Federation and the cantons are mindful of their responsibility to future generations.

(II) The Federation adopts regulations for the protection of the natural environment and to promote sustainable development.

(III) The Federation adopts regulations to protect the public from environmental dangers and to remedy their effects.

(IV) The realisation of environmental regulations is the responsibility of the cantons.

Article 91: Pollution

(I) The Federation adopts regulations to reduce pollution and to remedy its effects.

(II) The Federation adopts regulation to ensure the protection of water supplies from pollution.

(III) The realisation of pollution regulation is the responsibility of the cantons.

Article 92: Energy Infrastructure

(I) The Federation and the cantons aim to develop an efficient, economically viable, and environmentally sustainable energy supply.

(II) The Federation may support energy technology, in particular, the development of renewable energy.

(III) The Federation takes the needs, economic capabilities, and environmental diversity of the cantons into account in its energy policy.

Article 93: Protection of Heritage

(I) Protection of natural and cultural heritage is the responsibility of the cantons.

(II) The Federation may adopt regulations for the protection of natural and cultural heritage if they are required for the protection of public interest.

(III) The Federation and the cantons attempt to preserve objects of national importance.

Article 94: Animal Welfare

(I) The Federation adopts regulations on the keeping, care, use, trade, transport, breeding, and killing of animals.

(II) The Federation regulates to prevent the abuse and unnecessary suffering of animals.

(III) The Federation adopts regulations on fishing and hunting, in particular with regard for natural diversity and animal welfare.

Article 95: Road Network

(I) Maintenance of the road network is the responsibility of the cantons.

(II) The Federation adopts regulations on road traffic and goods transport.

(III) The Federation may adopt regulations to ensure the standardisation of the national road network and cooperation between cantons on road construction and maintenance.

Article 96: Public Transport

(I) The Federation and the cantons support the development and operation of public transport.

(II) The regulation of rail transport and aviation is the responsibility of the Federation.

Article 97: Footpaths

(I) The cantons are responsible for maintaining footpath networks.

(II) The Federation may support the maintenance and standardization of footpath networks.

(III) The state is conscious of the impact of footpath access on wildlife and agriculture.

Article 98: Postal Service

(I) The Federation establishes and operates a federal postal service.

(II) The federal postal service holds a monopoly on the production of national stamps.

Article 99: Television and Radio

(I) Regulation of television and radio is the responsibility of the Federation.

(II) The Federation and the cantons may establish public broadcasting services.

(III) In establishing public broadcasting services, the Federation and the cantons are conscious of freedom of the press.

Section 4- Finance, Economy, and Social Provisions

Article 100: Federal Budget

(I) The federal budget is drawn up for each each financial term. The duration of a financial term is determined by federal law.

(II) The Federation may not loan money to or borrow money from other states without a basis in federal law.

Article 101: Personal Taxation

(I) The Federation and the cantons may establish systems of personal taxation.

(II) Personal taxation is paid on a voluntary basis.

(III) Systems of personal taxation shall be conscious of economic needs and capabilities. They shall attempt to maximise citizens' choice.

Article 102: Further Taxation

(I) The Federation and the cantons may establish taxes on economic activity.

(II) In introducing further taxation, the Federation and the cantons are conscious of encouraging economic growth, protecting of natural resources, and the promoting economic equality.

Article 103: Banking and Investment

(I) The Federation establishes the Federal Bank of Francisville as the federal reserve.

(II) The Federation adopts regulations on private banking and investments.

(III) The Federal Bank of Francisville distributes a minimum of sixty per cent of its net profits to the cantons in a manner determined by federal law.

Article 104: National Currency

(I) The Federal Bank of Francisville holds the monopoly on the issue of the national currency.

(II) The power to issue the national currency may be delegated to publically controlled cantonal banks by means of a federal statute.

(III) The delegation of currency issue to private financial institutions is prohibited.

Article 105: Foreign Trade and Customs Duties

The regulation of foreign trade and customs duties is the responsibility of the Federation.

Article 107: Worker and Consumer protection

(I) The Federation adopts regulations for the protection of workers and consumers.

(II) The Federation and cantons adopts regulations to provide for legal action against fraudulance, deception, and damage to life and health caused by private enterprise.

(III) The Federation and the cantons ensure workers participation in themanagement of public services.

(IV) The Federation may adopt regulations in the domains of labour conditions and social security in pursuit of state social aims.

Article 108: Essential Goods and Services

(I) Economic policy ensures the supply of life essetial goods and services, particularly during periods of natural disaster.

(II) The Federation may nationalise and create public monopolies over essential goods and services in the persuit of state social aims.

Section 5- Civil and Criminal Law

Article 109: Civil Law

(I) The Federation adopts codified regulations on civil law and civil proceedure.

(II) The organisation and management of the court system is the responsibility of the cantons.

Article 110: Criminal Law

(I) The Federation adopts codified regulations on criminal law and criminal proceedure.

(II) The execution of criminal justice and penalties is the responsibility of the cantons, unless stated otherwise by federal law.

Article 111: Penalties and Punishment

(I) The Federation may aid the cantons in implementing criminal law and criminal penalties.

(II) Criminal law ensures that adequate material evidence and testimony is required throughout criminal proceedings. It mandates the need for expert opinion in proceedings where necessary.

(III) Criminal punishment shall be proportional to the severity of the crime, and be conscious of the weight of mitigating circumstances.

(IV) Criminal law conforms to the principles of restorative justice.

Article 112: Aid to Victims and Offenders

(I) The Federation and the cantons aim to provide aid to the victims of crime and to compensate them for any suffering or loss.

(II) The Federation and the cantons aim to aid the reintergration of offenders into society.

Title 4 – Federal Community

Article 113: Federal Community

(I) The Federal Community is the supreme legislative authority of the Federation. It comprises the Cantons and the entire voting population.

(II) Federal law is composed of all acts of legislation approved by the people and the cantons by the process of federal referendum.

Article 114: Acts of Legislation

(I) The Federal Chamber works with the people and the cantons in drafting acts of legislation, in particular to ensure their conformity with public demand.

(II) No two votes on the same proposal shall take place within 28 days of one another.

Article 115: Referendum

(I) Federal referendums are initiated and organised by the Federal Chamber.

(II) The referendum process is regulated by federal law in accordance with the Federal Constitution.

Article 116: Federal Refendum

(I) On the demand of at least one fifth of eligible voters within 28 days of the publication of the proposal, the Federal Chamber is obligated to submit the following to the people and the cantons:

a) Proposals for the admendment or repeal of a law.

b) Proposed acts of legislation.

(II) On the demand of at least one fifth of eligible voters within 28 days of their publication, the following are submitted to the people:

a) International treaties and agreements.

b) The appointment and reappointment of justices to the federal courts.

(III) On the demand for a referendum, the Federal Chamber shall organise it within 28 days.

Article 117: Cantonal Referendum

(I) On the demand of one fifth of eligible voters within the canton with 28 days ofthe publication of the proposal, a canton is obligated to submit the following are submitted to the people:

a) Statutes not initiated by popular vote.

b) Amendments to the cantonal constitution.

c) International and intercantonal treaties and agreements.

(II) On demand of a referendum, the canton shall organise it within 28 days.

Article 118: Required Majorities

(I) Proposals submitted to the people are accepted if approved by the majority of participating voters.

(II) Proposals submitted to the people and the cantons are accepted if approved by the majority of participating voters in the majority of cantons.

(III) If no votes are received from a canton, its vote is disregarded.

Title 5 – Federal Authorities

Chapter 1- Federal Government

Section 1- Election and Organisation

Article 120: Federal Government

(I) The Federal Government is comprised of the members of the Federal Council and the Federal Administration.

(II) The Federal Government is responsible for the execution of all tasks

delegated to the Federation, in accordance with the Federal Constitution and federal law.

Article 121: Federal Council

(I) The Federal Council is the highest executive authority of the Federation

(II) The Federal Council is composed of at least three members. It is composed of five members when the population exceeds twenty-five people. It is composed of seven members when the population exceeds forty people.

(III) The Federal Council is elected by the method of the Single Transferable Vote. The length of a term is defined by federal law.

Article 122: Federal President

(I) The Federal Council elects the Federal President and the Federal Vice-President from amongst its members for the duration of its term.

(II) The Federal President chairs the Federal Council. The Federal Vice-President exercises the duties of the Federal President in their absense.

(III) It is prohibited for the offices of the Federal President or the Federal Vice-President to be held by the same person for more than two terms consecutively. An outgoing Federal President may not be elected to the office of the Federal Vice-President.

Article 123: Collective Responsibility

(I) The Federal Council exercises the role of head of state of the Federation collectively.

(II) The members of the Federal Council share collective responsibility and exercise their duties as a collective unit.

Article 124: Immunity

(I) Members of the Federal Council enjoy legal immunity for all acts carried out in their official capacity.

(II) For crimes carried out outwith their official capacity prosecution of a Federal Councillor is permitted with the approval of majority of their colleagues.

Section 2- Powers and Responsibilities

58

Article 125: Federal Administration

(I) The Federal Council directs the Federal Administration

(II) The Federal Administration is divided into Federal Departments. Each Federal Department is directed by one member of the Federal Council.

(III) The Federal Administration consists of the Federal Departments and their

associated subordinate units. It performs its tasks in accordance with federal law as directed by the Federal Council.

Article 126: Foreign Relations and Treaties

(I) The Federal Council is responsible for the representation of Francisville abroad. It does so collectively or through a delegated member acting as its representative.

(II) The Federal Council signs foreign treaties and agreements collectively in accordance with foreign policy.

Article 127: National Security

(I) The Federal Council is responsible for coordinating national security.

(II) The Federal Council may mobilise an established militia in urgent circumstances within the limits of federal law and international agreements.

Article 128: Finances

(I) The Federal Council is responsible for the financial organisation of the Federaion and the federal accounts.

(II) The Federal Council submits its proposed federal budget to the Federal Chamber at the start of each fiscal term.

Article 129: Relations with the Cantons

(I) The Federal Council coordinates relations between the Federation and the cantons. It consults them on its policy and ensures the preservation of open relations.

(II) The Federal Council may raise objections against Cantons with regards to the Federal Constitution, federal law, and international and intercantonal agreements.

Chapter 2- Federal Chamber

Section 1- Organisation

Article 130: Status

(I) The Federal Chamber is the supreme representative body of the people.

(II) The authority of the Federal Chamber is subordinate to the authority of the Federal Community.

Article 131: Composition and Election

(I) The Federal Chamber is directly elected for a term of four months by the method of the single transferable vote.

(II) Each Canton constitutes an electoral district.

(III) Every Canton receives at least one deputy. The Cantons receive additional deputies in proportion to their population as regulated by federal law.

Article 132: President of the Chamber

(I) The Chamber elects a President as its presiding officer.

(II) The President appoints the Vice-Presidents. The Federal Chamber confirms the appointments.

Article 133: Parliamentary Committees

(I) The Federal Chamber establishes parliamentary committees. The organization of parliamentary committees is regulated by the Rules of Procedure.

(II) The parliamentary committees scrutinise proposed Acts of Legislation. They have the right to conduct inquiries and consultations as regulated by the Rules of

Procedure.

(III) All deputies have the right to join parliamentary committees. They have the right to join more than one committee.

Article 134: Parliamentary Groups

(I) Deputies have the right to organise themselves into parliamentary groups.

(II) The organisations of Parliamentary Groups is regulated by the Rules of Procedure.

Article 135: Standing Committees

(I) The Federal Chamber may establish Standing Committees to fulfill its

functions when it is not in session. The extent of their authority is regulated bythe Federal Chamber.

(II) Standing Committees shall be chaired by the President or a Vice-President of

the Federal Chamber.

Section 2- Procedure

Article 136: Rules of Procedure

The Federal Chamber adopts codified Rules of Procedure.

Article 137: Sessions

(I) The Federal Chamber meets for sessions regularly in a manner determined by its Rules of Procedure. It meets at least twice per term.

(II) The President of the Federal Chamber, a Federal Councillor, or one fourth of the deputies may demand a session.

(III) Sessions of the Federal Chamber are public. Exceptions require a basis in federal law or the rules of procedure.

Article 138: Quorum and majority

(I) The Federal Chamber require a fifty percent turnout of deputies for a quorum.

(II) All proposals in the Federal Chamber are passed if approved by the majority of voting deputies unless the Federal Constitution provides for exceptions.

Article 139: Right to Initiative

All deputies, members of the Federal Council, every parliamentary group, every parliamentary committee, and every canton through its political process has the right to submit proposals to the Federal Chamber.

Section 3- Functions

Article 140: Acts of Legislation

(I) The Federal Chamber is responsible for the deliberation and drafting of all proposed acts of legislation. It submits all proposals to the Federal Community.

(II) The Legislative Code is regulated by federal law. The Federal Chamber ensures that all proposed acts of legislation are drafted in a correct legal format.

Article 141: Foreign Relations

(I) The Federal Chamber approves international treaties and agreements.

(II) The Federal Chamber participates in the formation of foreign policy in cooperation with the Federal Council and the Federal Community.

Article 142: Budget and Finances

(I) The Federal Chamber approves the Federal Budget.

(II) The Federal Chamber examines the revenues and expenditures of the

Federation, It has the right to scrutinise the financial activities of all federal bodies.

Article 143: Supervision and Scrutiny

(I) The Federal Chamber scrutinises the activities of the Federal Government, the

Federal Courts, and all other federal bodies. It may hold inquiries into their proceedings and evaluate their efficiency.

(II) The Federal Chamber ensures that the activities of the Cantons conform to the Federal Constitution and federal law.

(III) The Federal Chamber regulates the procedure of the Federal Community.

Article 144: Relations with the Cantons

(I) The Federal Chamber facilitates relations between the Federation and the cantons. In particular, it involves the cantons in its decision making process.

(II) The Federal Chamber approves treaties and agreements between the cantons, and between the cantons and foreign states.

Article 144: Dissolution

(I) The majority of deputies may demand the dissolution of the Federal Chamber.

(II) A dissolution of the Federal Council shall coincide with a dissolution of the Federal Chamber. One may not be dissolved without the dissolution of the other.

(III) Elections shall be held no later than 28 days following a dissolution.

Article 146: Further Powers

Federal law may delegate further powers to the Federal Chamber.

Chapter 3- Federal Supreme Court

Article 147: Federal Supreme Court

(I) The Federal Supreme Court is the highest judicial authority in the Federation.

(II) The Federal Supreme Court has jurisdiction over matters related to the

following:

a) Federal law and the Federal Constitution

b) International treaties and agreements

c) Relations between Cantons and between the Federation and the Cantons

d) Complaints against the Federal Authorities

(III) Federal law may delegate further jurisdiction to the Federal Supreme Court.

Article 148: Governance of the Federal Supreme Court

(I) The Federal Supreme Court adopts rules of procedure for its governance.

(II) The members of the Federal Supreme Court are appointed by the Federal Council for a term of one year.

(III) The members of the Federal Supreme Court elect the Chief Justice from amongst their members. The Chief Justice serves as the President of the Supreme Court.

Article 149: Access to the Federal Supreme Court

(I) The Federation regulates to ensure access to the Federal Supreme Court.

(II) The proceedings of the Federal Supreme Court are public unless exceptions

are provided for by federal law for the protection of fundamental rights and freedoms or the efficient administration of the court.

Article 150: Interpretation and Scrutiny

(I) The Federal Supreme Court scrutinises the Federal Council, the Federal Chamber, and all proposed acts of legislation.

(II) The Federal Supreme Court vetos all acts of legislation submitted to the Federal Community which conflict with the Federal Constitution unless the proposals are concerning its revision.

Article 151: Further Federal Courts

(I) Federal law may establish further federal courts.

(II) Military jurisdiction over the courts is prohibited.

Article 152: Cantonal Courts

(I) The cantons establish their own judicial systems. The cantonal courts are responsible for the implementation of criminal and civil law in the cantons.

(II) The cantons have the right to establish intercantonal courts. The

establishment of intercantonal courts is subject to the same procedure as the implementation of intercantonal treaties.

Article 153: Separation of Powers

The Federation and the cantons ensure the political independence of the judicial authorities.

Title 6 – Amendments and Revision of the Constitution

Article 154: Partial Revision of the Constitution

(I) A partial revision of the Federal Constitution may be demanded by the Federal Community or by the Federal Council or the Federal Chamber.

(II) When a partial revision of the constitution is proposed, the Federal Chamber takes the appropriate measures.

(III) A partial revision of the constitution must preserve the unity oft he subject matter of the consitution. The Federal Chamber ensures that the provisions of articles not to be amended are unaffected.

Article 155: Full Revision of the Constitution

(I) A full revision of the Federal Constitution may be demanded by one third of eligible voters, one fourth of the cantons, the Federal Council, or the Federal Chamber.

(II) No two proposals for a full revision of the Federal Constitution may be submitted within six months of one another.

(III) When a full revision is proposed, the people decide on the manner of the revision. The provisions of the actual constitution are upheld.

Article 156: Required Constitutional Majorities

(I) Proposals for the amendment or revision of the Federal Constitution require an absolute majority in favour in the Federal Chamber.

(II) Proposals for the amendment or revision of the Federal Constitution require

an absolute majority of the population or a two-thirds majority of voters in support in a federal referendum.

(III) Proposals for the amendment of revision of the Federal Constitution require the support of the majority of voters in the majority of Cantons.

Article 157: Principles Guaranteed in Perpetuity

(I) Revisions to the Federal Constitution, both full and partial, which threaten the secular, democratic, republican or federal nature of the state are prohibited.

(II) Revisions to the Federal Constitution shall preserve the general essence of fundamental human rights.

Legislative Code
A CODE TO ESTABLISH STANDARDS BY WHICH LEGISLATION IS TO ABIDE

SECTION I – Legal Provisions

Article 1 – Short Title

This Code may be cited as the Legislative Code or abbreviated as LC. Where need be distinguished, it may be cited as the Legislative Code (Francisville) or abbreviated as LC (FRV).

Article 2 – Duration

This Code shall come into effect immediately upon its approval by the Federal Community of Francisville and shall be valid in its current form until it is revoked or amended by an institution that has the power to do so given either by the Constitution, this Code or further legislation.

Article 3 – Definitions

Within the context of this code,

LEGISLATION shall refer to "any item of federal law drafted by the Federal Chamber and approved by the people of Francisville";

Article 4 – Purpose

The purpose of this code is to avoid misinterpretations of and ambiguities within the law, as well as improving its comprehensibility for the Francillian people and generally facilitating its implementation and use.

SECTION II – Basic Structure of Legislation

Article 5 – Chapters, Sections and Subsections

5.1 All legislation must be divided at least into sections, which contain individual articles.

5.2 Legislation that fulfills or exceeds 3000 words in length (including also titles and pro forma content) may be further divided into two or more chapters, which contain the sections.

5.3 Legislation that fulfills or exceeds 6000 words in length (including also titles and pro forma content) and is already divided into chapters may be further divided into subsections, which are contained in the sections. If a section has no content outwith subsections, it must have either at least two subsections or none at all. If it does have content outwith subsections, it may have only one subsection.

5.4 Sections and chapters are ascendingly designated Roman numerals. Subsections are ascendingly designated uppercase letters of the Latin alphabet. If the Latin alphabet is exhausted, the Greek alphabet may be used.

5.5 The ongoing count of a division is reset upon exiting the higher-level division that it is part of (a

Section IX in Chapter II is followed by a Section I in Chapter III).

5.6 Articles are ascendingly designated Western Arabic numerals. The ongoing count of articles is not reset within one item of legislation.

Article 6 – Division of Articles

6.1 Articles may be subdivided into paragraphs, clauses and subclauses. An article may have clauses despite having no paragraphs, but may not have subclauses despite having no clauses.

6.2 Paragraphs are indicated by the article number, followed by a period, followed by an ascending Western Arabic numeral that resets for every article.

6.3 Clauses are indicated by an opening bracket, followed by an ascending lowercase letter of the Latin alphabet, followed by a closing bracket. The clause count resets for every paragraph or, if none, for every article

6.4 Subclauses are indicated by a lowercase ascending Roman numeral, followed by a period. The subclause count resets for every clause.

Article 7 – Mandatory Subjects

7.1 All legislation must possess:

(a) A common short title, listed at the very top of the legislation document,

(b) A long (also known as proper) title, listed beneath the common short title at the top of the respective piece of legislation in uppercase.

(c) An abbreviation for use in referencing as per §10. 7.2 The following sections must exist within all legislation:

(a) A section titled "Legal Provisions" (see §8), regarding legal provisions concerning the legislation. This section must be the first section of the respective piece of legislation.

(b) A section titled "Treatment" (see §9), regarding the validity of the respective piece of legislation with regards to authorities and the whole of Francillian law. This section must be the final section of the respective piece of legislation.

Article 8 – Legal Provisions

8.1 The "Legal Provisions" section is to contain the articles "Short Title", "Duration", "Definitions" and "Purpose".

8.2 The article "Short Title" details the short forms and abbreviations that are legally sound to be used for referring to the piece of legislation in question. It may also allow for disambiguative forms and abbreviations.

8.3 The article "Duration" details the date at which the respective piece of legislation becomes valid and affirms the dependence of the legislation's validity on further regulations by itself, other legislation, or authorised institutions within the limits of the Constitution.

8.4 The article "Definitions" defines any terms that occur in the respective piece of legislation that

require clarification, be it due to ambiguity, originality, or diversion from the usual meaning of the term.

8.5 The article "Purpose" defines the intended practical purpose of the act. This is distinguished from the long title of the respective piece of legislation in that the purpose defines what the intended practical effect of the respective piece of legislation is, as opposed to the direct, abstract purpose given by the long title.

Article 9 – Treatment

9.1 The "Treatment" section is to contain the articles "Expiry", "Amendments" and "Prioritisation".

9.2 The article "Expiry" details specific times and circumstances at which the respective piece of legislation expires, or states that it does not have any terms of expiration.

9.3 The article "Amendments" details which institutions, apart from the Federal Chamber with the Federal Community, may have the authorisation to amend the respective piece of legislation, if applicable. It may further give required circumstances for amendments to be permissible, such as a non-vacancy of the position of President of the Chamber, or at least a year having gone by since the original passing or last amendment of the respective piece of legislation.

9.4 The article "Prioritisation" details what is to take place should the respective piece of legislation conflict with either existing or new legislation.

Article 10 – Referencing

10.1 Items within pieces of legislation are cited as follows: §a.p(c) L, where a is the article number, p the paragraph number, c the letter corresponding to the clause, s the numeral corresponding to the subclause, and L the abbreviation of the respective piece of legislation. Thus, article 7 paragraph 2 clause a of this code would be cited as §7.2(a) LC.

10.2 Subclauses cannot be directly referenced, therefore, they should not be used in a way that could require them to.

10.3 The abbreviation of the respective piece of legislation can be omitted if it is clear which piece of legislation is meant.

10.4 Ranges of items can be indicated with hyphens, eg. §7-9 indicating articles 7 to 9, or §5.4-6 to indicate article 5 paragraphs 4 to 6.

Article 11 – Formatting

11.1 The preferred font for legislation is Cambria. Other serif fonts, such as Centaur, Garamond, Minion or Times New Roman, may be used only if Cambria is not available.

11.2 All formatting instructions below are exact, i.e. if no mention of boldface is made, boldface is prohibited, not optional. If no case (all-capitals, title case etc) is given, assume ordinary English capitalisation rules.

11.3 The common short title at the top of the respective piece of legislation is to be formatted in 14pt boldface.

11.4 The long title appearing after the common short title at the top of the respective piece of legislation must be formatted in 12pt all-capitals.

11.5 Section headings must be formatted in 13pt boldface, with the text "section" being capitalised, followed by the numeral indicating the section, followed by space, en-dash, space and the section name in title case.

11.6 Starting from the first section heading, there must be 6pt of additional space after each line (this can be done in the "paragraph" settings of most word processors. This can be omitted from blank lines for aesthetic purposes.

11.7 Article headings must be formatted in 12pt boldface, with the text "Article", followed by the article number, followed by space, en-dash, space and the article name in title case.

11.8 Paragraph indicators must be formatted in 12pt boldface.

11.9 Ordinary text must be formatted in 12pt.

11.10 Clause indicators must be indented by 0.53 cm, with the text following them having a hanging indentation of 0.83 cm.

11.11 Subclause indicators must be indented by 1.06 cm, with the text following them having a hanging indentation of 1.36 cm.

Article 12 – Appendices

12.1 The creator of the legislation may append any relevant factual documents, such as outlines, plans, tables, projections, white papers, schemata, implementation regulations et al to the Act.

(a) These appended documents shall come under "Appendix A – Attached Documents" and must, digitally, be saved in separate files.

(b) Appendix A must be published and recorded along with the legislation itself in all official publications.

12.2 All members of the Federal Chamber, particularly those who were involved in drafting a certain piece of legislation, are entitled to append a document to the piece of legislation detailing their thoughts on it and, in the case of having drafted it, the motivation behind it.

(a) If appended by the person or entity putting the respective item of legislation to the Chamber, these appended documents shall come under "Appendix B – Justification".

(b) Appendix B may be published and recorded along with the legislation itself in any official publication.

(c) If appended by a person or entity other than those putting the respective item of legislation to the Chamber, these appended documents shall come under "Appendix C – Commentary".

(d) Appendix C must not be published or recorded along with the legislation itself in any official publications other than publications outlining the history/progression of the legislation through the Chamber, and especially not in publications of the law created for the purpose of its judiciary use.

12.3 Any other documents not accurately described in §12.1 and §12.2 of this Act may come under "Appendix D – Miscellaneous".

SECTION III – Terminology and Global Definitions

Article 13 – Titles

13.1 Pieces of legislation termed "Act" have a subject matter of an immediate, temporary, or very specific nature.

(a) Acts may be replaced by newer acts with an identical title and thus must specify the year in which they were passed in their short title.

(b) If more than one Act with an identical short title is passed in one year, a Roman numeral is interfixed between the name of the Act and the word "Act", i.e. Example (II) Act, 2012.

13.2 Pieces of legislation termed "Code" have a subject matter of a generic and permanent nature. No two Codes may have the same subject matter or identical short or long titles, nor can one Code supersede another.

13.3 Pieces of legislation termed "Resolution" are decisions or plans of action that, once executed, are no longer legally relevant bar for occurrences at the time they were still in the process of being executed. Resolutions may have identical short and long titles and can supersede one another. Resolutions are numbered incrementally, starting from 1 for the first resolution passed by the

Federal Chamber.

13.4 Pieces of legislation termed "Regulation" concern government administrative matters and are the only type of legislation that can be issued by any government organ independently of the Federal Chamber. Regulations can be revoked by the Federal Chamber or the Federal Supreme Court, and a federal government agency's right to issue regulations can be revoked by the Federal

Community.

13.5 Where conflicts between items of legislation exist,

(a) Codes supersede all other forms of legislation,

(b) Acts supersede regulations and resolutions, but are subordinate to codes,

(c) Regulations supersede resolutions, but are subordinate to codes and acts,

(d) Resolutions are subordinate to all other forms of legislation.

13.6 The short title of a piece of legislation must represent the subject matter of the respective piece of legislation in brief, while the long title must delineate the immediate goal of the respective piece of legislation within a legal context. Both titles must be accurate to the content of the respective piece of legislation.

13.7 The President of the Federal Council retains the right to deem the title of a piece of legislation that has not yet passed inaccurate, inadequate or misleading, and may thus alter the titles of the respective piece of legislation to descriptions they find to be more appropriate.

Article 14 – Sensibility of Definition

Definitions given in the "Definitions" article of a respective piece of legislation may not differ from the dictionary definition or implied etymological meaning of a term to an extent at which the term as defined in the respective piece of legislation appears to be unrelated to the term in common use.

Article 15 – Global Definitions

The following definitions are definitions valid for all pieces of legislation, unless contradicted by the definitions given in the "Definitions" article of the respective piece of legislation:

15.1 FRANCISVILLE refers to "the Federal Republic of Francisville".

15.2 FRANCILLIAN GOVERNMENT refers to "the Government of FRANCISVILLE".

15.3 THE FEDERAL CHAMBER refers to "the Federal Chamber of FRANCISVILLE", unless in grammatical reference to another chamber specified earlier on.

15.4 THE FEDERAL COUNCIL refers to "the Federal Council of FRANCISVILLE", unless in grammatical reference to another chamber specified earlier on.

15.5 THE FEDERAL COMMUNITY refers to "the Federal Community of FRANCISVILLE", unless in grammatical reference to another chamber specified earlier on.

15.6 THE FEDERAL SUPREME COURT refers to "the Federal Supreme Court of FRANCISVILLE".

15.7 THE LAW refers to "the collection of all pieces of legislation currently valid in FRANCISVILLE".

15.8 THE CONSTITUTION refers to "the Constitution of FRANCISVILLE", unless in grammatical reference to another constitution specified earlier on.

15.9 THE FEDERATION refers to "the Federal-level FRANCILLIAN GOVERNMENT".

15.10 THE CANTONS refers to "the individual cantons of FRANCISVILLE".

15.11 DEPUTY refers to "a deputy to the FEDERAL CHAMBER".

SECTION IV – Implementation and Accountability

Article 19 – The Drafter

19.1 Any member of the Federal Chamber who drafts a piece of legislation is responsible for ensuring that the respective piece of legislation abides in full to every provision of this code.

19.2 If the President of the Federal Chamber notices that a certain member of the Federal Chamber consistently neglects to abide by the Legislative Code, they must penalise the respective member. If, after being penalised accordingly, that member continues to ignore this code, the President may call a vote to have said member's right to draft legislation temporarily revoked.

Article 19 – The President of the Federal Chamber

20.1 The President of the Federal Chamber is responsible for ascertaining that each item of legislation drafted by members of the Federal Chamber adheres to the regulations set out in this code, as well as being otherwise unambiguous and employing correct orthography and grammar.

20.2 If the President of the Federal Chamber fails to notice violations of this code in a piece of legislation before said piece of legislation is passed, but notices that this is the case after the respective piece of legislation has been passed, they must submit a memorandum of error to the Chief Justice.

20.3 Upon receiving a memorandum of error from the President of the Federal Chamber, the Chief Justice must rule on whether or not the piece of legislation referred to in the memorandum is to be invalidated. If so, it is sent back to the Federal Chamber for review and editing to the end of compatibilising it to this code, then resubmitting the respective piece of legislation in its adjusted form to the Federal Community for voting.

20.4 A single holder of the Presidency of the Federal Chamber may not submit multiple memoranda of error concerning the same respective piece of legislation.

20.5 If the Chief Justice finds that the incumbent President of the Federal Chamber is misusing their power of submitting memoranda of errors, the Federal Chamber must remove its incumbent President from office and hold another election for the position. The dismissed President may, however, stand for re-election in such a mandated election.

Article 21 – Members of the Federal Chamber

While Members of the Federal Chamber are not obligated to proofread any pieces of legislation they did not draft themselves for compliance with this code, any such Member who does find a violation against code in such legislation is obligated to inform both the Drafter and the Speaker of this immediately.

Article 22 – Judicial Review

22.1 Judges at any court of any level, federal or cantonal, may file a memorandum of error with the Chief Justice should they find during a trial that a piece of legislation does not abide by the regulations of this code.

22.2 Upon receiving a memorandum of error from a judge, the Chief Justice must rule on whether or not the piece of legislation referred to in the memorandom is to be invalidated. If so, it is sent back to the Federal Chamber for review and editing to the end of compatibilising it to this code, then resubmitting the respective piece of legislation in its adjusted form to the Federal Community for voting.

22.3 If a memorandum of error originating from a judge results in a piece of legislation being invalidated, the Federal Chamber must remove its incumbent President from office and hold another election for the position. The dismissed President may, however, stand for re-election in such a mandated election.

Article 23 – Citizen Review

Any citizen who finds that a piece of legislation does not abide by the regulations of this code may petition the lowest-level judge with jurisdiction over said citizen's area to review the respective piece of legislation and file a memorandum of error with the Chief Justice according to the procedure laid out in §22 of this code.

SECTION V – Treatment

Article 24 – Expiry

There is no set limit on the legal validity of this code.

Article 25 – Amendments

Amendments to this code can be proposed by the Federal Chamber and must be voted on by the Federal Community.

Article 26 – Prioritisation

Where this code conflicts with other legislation of its own level as per §13.1-5 of this code, the determinations that have most recently been accepted by the Federal Community take precedence. This includes entirely new documents as well as amendments. Legislation below its own level is irrelevant to the validity of the code. Any violations of the constitution are legally null and void and not legally effective.

Freedonia

Constitution

Constitution of the Principality of Freedonia

This document is the supreme and highest law of the Principality of Freedonia.

Preamble

The aim of all political association is the preservation of the natural and imprescriptible rights of man. These rights are liberty, security in person and property, and resistance to oppression. We feel that present day governments are no longer effective protectors of the rights and liberties of the people. So we hereby establish this constitution to ensure the liberty of the people and let people live free in the Principality of Freedonia.

We hold that the principles contained in this Preamble should be the beacon of the Principality and thus take precedence over all other laws of the land, including Articles contained in this Constitution. Therefore the People of the Sovereign Principality of Freedonia recognize and proclaim, in the presence and under the auspices of the Creator, the following rights of Man and of the Citizen, that:

All persons are born free and remain free and equal in rights. Social distinctions are an economic necessity. In no way are anyone's rights related to their economic status.

Liberty consists in the freedom to do everything which injures no one else, nor anyone's property; hence the exercise of the natural rights of each man has no limits except those which assure to the

other members of the society the enjoyment of the
same rights.

 The Prince and the Parliament shall make no law respecting an
establishment of religion, or prohibiting the free exercise thereof;
or abridging the freedom of speech, or of the press; or the right of
the people peaceably to assemble, and to petition the Government
for a redress of grievances.

 Being necessary to the security of a free State, the right of the
people to keep and bear Arms, shall not be infringed.

 No Soldier shall, in time of peace be quartered in any house,
without the consent of the Owner, nor in time of war, but in a
manner to be prescribed by law.

 The right of the people to be secure in their persons, houses,
papers, and effects, against unreasonable searches and seizures,
shall not be violated, and no Warrants shall issue, but upon
probable cause, supported by Oath or affirmation, and particularly
describing the place to be searched, and the persons or things to be
seized.

 No person shall be held to answer for a capital, or otherwise
infamous crime, unless on a presentment or indictment of a Grand
Jury, except in cases arising in the land or naval forces, or in the
Militia, when in actual service in time of War or public danger; nor
shall any person be subject for the same offense to be twice put in
jeopardy of life or limb; nor shall be compelled in any criminal
case to be a witness against himself, nor be deprived of life,
liberty, or property, without due process of law; nor shall private
property be taken for public use, without just compensation. As all
persons are held innocent until they shall have been declared
guilty, if arrest shall be deemed indispensable, all harshness not
essential to the securing of the prisoner's person shall be severely
repressed by law.

In all criminal prosecutions, the accused shall enjoy the right to a speedy and public trial, by an impartial jury, and to be informed of the nature and cause of the accusation; to be confronted with the witnesses against him; to have compulsory process for obtaining witnesses in his favor, and to have the Assistance of Counsel for his defense.

For criminals, the law shall provide for such punishments only as are strictly and obviously necessary, and no one shall suffer punishment except it be legally inflicted in virtue of a law passed.

The security of the rights of man and of the citizen requires military forces. These forces are, therefore, established for the good of the nation and not for the advantage of any one person.

Law is the expression of the general good. Every citizen has a right to participate personally, through petitioning his representative, through petitioning the Prince, and through initiative in its foundation. Laws must be the same for all, whether it protects or punishes. All citizens over age 15, being equal in the eyes of the law, are equally eligible to all dignities and to all government positions and government occupations, according to their abilities, and without distinction except that of their virtues and talents.

The enumeration in the Constitution, of certain rights, shall not be construed to deny or disparage others retained by the people.

The powers not delegated to the government by the Constitution, nor prohibited by it, are reserved
to the people.

Article I. Legislative Powers

Section 1.

All legislative powers herein granted shall be vested solely in the Parliament of Freedonia, but the People reserve unto themselves the powers of initiative and recall.

Section 2. The Parliament; how elected; terms.

(a) The Parliament shall be composed of members chosen at large for two years by the People of Freedonia.

(b) No person shall be a member of Parliament who has not attained the age of 15, and who when elected
shall not be a Citizen of Freedonia.

(c)The initial enumeration of seats in Parliament shall be 10. An additional 5 seats shall be created per 2500 citizens until Parliament reaches 30 seats.

(d) When vacancies happen in the representation of the Parliament, the Prime Minister shall appoint a Citizen otherwise fulfilling the requirements of Article I, Section 2(b) to serve for the remainder of the unexpired term for that seat.

(e) The Prime Minister of Freedonia shall be the Head of the Parliament but shall have no vote unless they be equally divided.

(f) The Parliament shall choose their officers and also a head of parliament in the absence of the Prime Minister.

(g) The Parliament shall assemble least once each year and such meeting shall take place at a time and place as they shall appoint by law.

Section 3. Oath of office

Before elected members of Parliament enter on the Execution of their Offices, they shall take the following Oath:-- iI do solemnly swear that I will well and faithfully execute the duties of the office on which I am about to enter, and will to the best of my Ability, preserve, protect and defend the Constitution of the Principality of Freedonia."

Section 4. Parliament and internal proceedings.

(a) The Parliament shall submit to the Electory Board to be the judge of elections, of its own members, and a majority shall constitute a quorum to do business but a smaller number may adjourn from day to day, and may be authorized to compel the attendance of absent members in such manner and under such penalties as it may provide.

(b) The Parliament may determine the rules of its proceedings, and from time to time publish the same excepting such parts as may in their judgment, and with the concurrence of the Prince, require secrecy; and the yeas and nays of the members on any question shall, at the desire of one-fifth of those present, be entered on the journal.

Section 5. Compensation; holding of other offices.

(a) The Parliament may receive compensation for their services to be determined by the will of the People through referendum.

(b) No member of Parliament shall, during the time for which he was elected, hold any other office under the authority of the Principality of Freedonia.

Section 6. Bills and Acts.

(a) Every bill originating in the Parliament shall, before it becomes a law, be presented to the Prince. If he approves he shall sign it, but if not he shall return it, with his objections to the Parliament who shall enter the objections at large in their journal, and proceed to reconsider it. If after reconsideration, four fifths of the

Parliament shall agree to pass the bill it shall become law. But in all such cases the votes shall be determined by yeas and nays and the names of the persons shall be entered on the journal of the Parliament. If any bill shall not be rejected by the Prince within 60 days after it shall be presented to him, the same shall be law in like manner as if he had signed it, unless the Parliament by their adjournment prevent its return, or unless the Prince is prevented physically from returning it by extraneous circumstances, in which case it shall not be law.

(b) Laws passed by parliament can be declared unconstitutional if the majority of Grand Council declares it to be so.

Section 7. Power of Impeachment

(a) The Parliament shall have the sole Power of Impeachment.

(b) The Parliament shall have the sole Power to try all Impeachments. When sitting for that Purpose, they shall be on Oath or Affirmation. And no Person shall be convicted without the Concurrence of two thirds of the Members present.

(c) Judgment in Cases of Impeachment shall not extend further than to removal from Office, and disqualification to hold and enjoy any Office of honor, Trust or Profit under Freedonia: but the Party convicted shall nevertheless be liable and subject to Indictment, Trial, Judgment and Punishment, according to Law.

Section 8. Powers of the Parliament.

The Parliament shall have the power

(a) to provide for punishment for counterfeiting the securities and current coin of the Principality;

(b) to fix the standard of weights and measures used by government;

(c) to promote the progress of science and useful arts by securing for limited times the exclusive right to their respective writings and discoveries;

(d) to define and punish piracies and felonies committed on the high seas,

(e) grant letters of marque and reprisal.

Section 9. Restrictions

(a) The naturalization of such persons as the Prince thinks proper shall not be prohibited.

(b) The privilege of the writ of habeas corpus shall not be suspended.

(c) No bill of attainder nor ex post facto law shall be passed.

(e) No money shall be drawn from the Treasury by Parliament but in consequence of appropriations made by law;

(f) All laws and bills passed by parliament shall relate solely to the establishment, structure, and operation of: the courts, the police, and other justice and law enforcement systems. Except:

(i) Laws and bills relating to the specific legislative powers outlined elsewhere in this article,

(ii) Laws and bills concerning taxation and the funding of constitutionally authorized operations of government

(iii) Laws enabling the enforcement of contracts, and;

(iv) Laws which define, or establish levels of punishment for, types of crimes and torts. An action can be considered a crime or tort only if it meets the following definitions:

A crime is any action taken by an individual wherein the individual intentionally initiates physical force, fraud, or theft which results in damage to another individual or damage or loss of another individual's property without the consent of that individual. Tort is any unintentional action that results in damage to another individual or damage or loss of another Individual's property.

Section 10.

The Parliament shall meet for no more than 5 consecutive weeks a year, unless a time extension be granted by the Prince.

Article II. The Prince.

Section 1.

The Princeís solemn duty is to act as a Supreme guardian of the Freedonian people, their rights, and their liberties. As the pinnacle of Freedonia, the Prince represents the best of Freedonian society, and is the proponent of freedom.

Section 2. Prince and how chosen.

(a) The Executive Power of the Principality insomuch as it relates to the internal governance of the Principality shall be vested in the Prince. The Prince shall be the advocate of the People.

(b) The Prince shall serve for life or until such time as he shall relinquish the Crown.

(c) Upon relinquishing the Crown, the Prince shall establish his successor without interference from any group or body. During his reign he may establish, at his leisure, a Prince Regent to serve in the event of his untimely death or disability.

Section 3. Prince to be Commander-in-Chief

(a) The Prince shall be the Commander-in-Chief of the army and navy and other armed forces of the Principality.

(b) The Prince shall commission all military officers of the Principality.

Section 4. The Powers of the Prince on behalf of the People shall be,

(a) to create a cabinet and appoint its members.

(b) to delegate his powers unto cabinet members and the ministries they may create as he sees fit, to appoint a member to the Electory Council, and to appoint the Minister of Defense to provide advice on the judicious use of the army and navy of the Principality on behalf of the People;

(c) to investigate the courts, the police, and other justice and law enforcement bodies in order to ensure their integrity, lack of corruption, and adherance to the law.

(d) to issue passports and other citizenship related documents

(e) to grant reprieves and pardons;

(f) to annex territory on behalf of the People of Freedonia;

(g) to coin money and regulate the value thereof,

(h) to bestow Royal titles, medals, or other rewards for outstanding service to the Principality

(i) to raise and support armies for the common defense, to provide and maintain a navy, to make rules for the government and regulation of the land, naval, and other forces and to provide for calling forth the militia to execute the
laws of the Principality, suppress insurrection, and repel invasions; to provide for organizing, arming, disciplining the militias and for governing such part of them as may be employed in the service of the Principality.

(j) to establish and administer the Royal Guard to serve for his protection and the excersising of his duties under this article.

(k) to represent Freedonia in all ambassadorial functions with foreign governments, and to negotiate and enter into treaties on Freedonia's behalf.

Section 4. Powers of the Prince relating to law.

The following Powers shall be irrevocably vested in the Prince in the interest
of the People;

(a) to propose laws and bills to be voted on by parliament

(b) to make official Royal Proclomations and Reccomendations on activities occuring within the Principality, although these do not carry the force of law.

(b) to call special referendums to determine the will of the People for his own information.

(c) to veto bills and laws passed by the parliament

(d) to have sole authority over all immigration and naturalization issues

(e) to designate official holidays, and to establish the flags, insignias, and symbols of Freedonia.

Section 5. Compensation

The Prince shall be compensated for general housing and living expenses, with any personal compensation to be determined through referendum or act of Parliament. The Prince shall also be funded as necessary for the carrying out of the duties with which he is charged under this article (except for fuding of the military, which shall be the domain of Parliament). The Prince shall submit annually a budget to this end, which shall be adopted unless rejected by 4/5 of the Parliament. In the event that funding is restricted in such a way as to undermine the ability of the Monarchy to fulfill its constitutional duties and obligations, the Grand Council may intervene in order to ensure the budget's assent.

Article III. The Prime Minister.

Section 1.

(a) The Administrative Power of the Principality shall be vested in the Prime Minister of Freedonia, in that he shall see to the logistical implementation of Parliamentary law. He shall hold his office for a term of two years and be elected as follows:

(b) Citizens having reached the age of majority as proscribed by law may vote. Under the supervision of the Electory Board without the Prime Minister, the ballots shall be tallied. The person having the greatest number of votes shall be Prime Minister, if such number be a majority of votes cast. If no person receives a majority of votes cast a special Election shall be called by the Prince for thirty days hence and the three persons receiving the greatest number of votes during the general election shall be placed on the ballot. The person receiving the greatest number of votes during the special election shall be the Prime Minister notwithstanding a majority of votes received.

(c) No person shall be Prime Minister who shall not have attained the age of majority as established by legislation at the time of his election and who, when elected, after the year 2001, shall not have been a citizen of Freedonia for a period of one year.

(d) In case of removal of the Prime Minister from office, or of his death, resignation, or inability to discharge the duties of the said office, the same shall devolve on the Secretary of Treasury, and in the case of removal, death, resignation, or inability of both Prime Minister and Secretary of Treasury, the Minister of Defense shall fulfill the duties of Prime Minister until the Prince shall call special election not less than 30 days nor more than 45 days after the vacancy occurs to fill the unexpired term of the office of the Prime Minister.

(e) The Prime Minister may receive compensation for their services in an amount to be determined by referendum of the people.

Section 2. Foreign matters

The Prime Minister shall have the power and duty of logistical administration of consulate and embassy offices abroad, as well as the managing of difficulties encountered by Freedonian citizens abroad.

Section 3. The Prime Minister shall communicate to the Parliament.

He shall from time to time give the Parliament information of the State of the Principality and recommend to their consideration such measures as he shall judge necessary and expedient; he shall take care that the laws be faithfully executed.

Section 4. All civil offices Forfeited for Certain crimes.

The Prime Minister, and all civil officers of the Principality shall be removed from office on impeachment for, and conviction of, treason, bribery, or other high crimes or misdemeanors. The Prince may not be impeached.

Section 5. Oath of office

Before the elected Prime Minister enters on the Execution of his Office, he shall take the following Oath:-- iI do solemnly swear that I will well and faithfully execute the duties of the office on which I am about to enter, and will to the best of my Ability, preserve, protect and defend the Constitution of the Principality of Freedonia."

Article IV. Judiciary.

Section 1. Judicial Powers.

(a) The judicial power of the Principality of Freedonia shall be vested in the Grand Council and in such Grand Juries as the People shall see fit to establish. The Justices of the Grand Council shall be five in number. One shall be elected by the people, one shall be selected by the Parliament, and the remaining three shall be chosen by the Prince. Justices shall serve for 3 years. The manner of electing Justices of the Grand Council shall be selected at large in the same fashion as for the Parliament.

(b) There shall be one Judge elected to each Grand Jury to serve a term of one year. The right to sentence is reserved to the Jury. The members of each Grand Jury established by the People shall be determined by the Judge
of said Jury drawing at random the names of twelve citizens.

(c) All judicial offices shall be non-partisan. No political party or party central committee may endorse, support, or oppose a candidate for judicial office.

Section 2. Judicial power; extent; original jurisdiction of Grand Council.

(a) The Judicial Power of the Grand Council shall extend to all cases in law and equity arising under this Constitution, the laws of the Principality, and treaties made, or which shall be made, under their authority; to all cases affecting ambassadors, other public ministers and consuls, and to all cases of admiralty and maritime jurisdiction.

(b) The Grand Council shall review every law originating from the Parliament to ensure that the law does not violate the constitution or violate the rights of Freedonian citizens. The Grand Council may declare a law unconstitutional, null, and void by a simple majority.

(b) In all cases affecting the Prince, ambassadors, other public ministers and consuls, and cases to which the Principality is a party, the Grand Council shall be the court of original jurisdiction.

In all other cases, The Grand Council shall have appellate jurisdiction.

(c) The trial of all crimes, except in cases of impeachment shall be by Grand Jury.

Section 3. Treason defined; proof of; punishment.

(a) Treason against the Principality of Freedonia shall consist only in levying war against it or in adhering to its enemies, giving them aid and comfort. No person shall be convicted of treason unless on the testimony of two witnesses to the overt act or on confession in open court.

(b) The Parliament shall have the power to declare the punishment of treason.

Article V. The Electory Council

Section 1.

The Electory council is responsible for holding elections and ensuring the accuracy and fairness of the tallying process.

Section 2.

(a) The Electory Council shall consist of a panel composed of 3 members. One member is the Prime Minister, one is elected by the Parliament, and one is appointed by the Prince.

(b) Each member of the Electory Council shall serve for a period of two years.

(c) The Prime Minister will not sit on the Electory Council when it concerns the election of the Prime Minister.

(d) In the election of the first Parliament, the Electory Council shall consist of the Prime Minister, an appointee by the Prince, and an indvidual elected by the public.

Article VI. Voting, Initiative, Referendum, and Recall

Section 1.

The Parliament shall prohibit improper practices that affect elections and shall provide for the disqualification of electors while mentally incompetent or imprisoned or on parole for the conviction of a felony.

Section 3. Initiative, how called.

(a) The initiative is the right of the People to propose statutes and amendments to the Constitution and to adopt or reject them.

(b) An initiative measure may be proposed by presenting to the Electory Board a petition that sets forth the text of the proposed statute or amendment to the Constitution and is certified to have been signed by electors equal in number to 5 percent in the case of a statute, and 8 percent in the case of an amendment to the Constitution, of the votes for all candidates for Prime Minister at the last election.

(c) The Electory Board shall then submit the measure at the next general election held at least 61 days after it qualifies or at any special election held prior to that general election. The Prince may call a special election for the measure.

(d) An initiative measure embracing more than one subject may not be submitted to the People or have any effect.

Section 4.

(a) An initiative statute or amendment approved by a majority of votes thereon is submitted to the Prince where if it is signed by the Prince, it becomes effective immediately. If it is not signed by the Prince, it is voted upon by the Parliament as a bill, subject to veto.

(b) If provisions of 2 or more measures approved at the same election conflict, those of the measure receiving the greatest number of affirmative votes shall prevail.

(c) The statute must be approved by majority of the Grand Council.

(d) Prior to circulation of an initiative or referendum petition for signatures, a copy shall be submitted to the Electory Board who shall prepare a title and summary of the measure as provided by law.

(e) The Parliament shall provide the manner in which petitions shall be circulated, presented, and certified, and measures submitted to the People.

Section 6.

No amendment to the Constitution, and no statute proposed to the People by the Parliament or by initiative, that names any individual to hold any office, or names or identifies any private corporation to perform any function or to have any power or duty, may be submitted to the People or have any effect. No bill of attainder may be passed.

Section 7. Recall; how determined; petitions.

(a) Recall of any elected civil officer is initiated by delivering to the Electory Board a petition alleging reason for recall. Sufficiency of reason is not reviewable. Proponents have 30 days to file signed petitions.

(b) A petition to recall an officer must be signed by eligible voters equal in number to 15 percent of the votes cast in the election for said officer.

(c) The Electory Board shall maintain a continuous count of the signatures certified to that office.

Section 8. Recall Elections.

(a) An election to determine whether to recall an officer and, if appropriate, to elect a successor shall be called by the Prince and held not less than 30 days nor more than 45 days from the date of certification of sufficient signatures.

(b) A recall election may be conducted within 90 days from the date of certification of sufficient signatures in order that the election may be consolidated with the next general election.

(c) If there is a majority vote of three fourths on the question is to recall, the officer is removed and, if there is a candidate, the candidate who receives a plurality is the successor. The officer may not be a candidate.

Section 9. The parliament shall provide for circulation, filing, and certification of petitions, nomination of candidates, and the recall election.

Article VII. Sovereign Territory and Annexation

The aquisition of sovereign territory being necessary for the establishment of Freedonia, the Prince shall have the authority to raise and appropriate funds for the aquisition of territory and other establishment expenses. All funds raised shall be on a voluntary basis. Once territory is acquired, any land initially owned by the Freedonian government is to be sold into private hands, with the proceeds to be allocated by the Prince to address start-up expenses.

Article VIII. Constitution; how amended.

Section 1

(a) The Prince may propose amendments to the constitution which shall then be included as part of this Constitution on the ratification of such amendment by one half of the People, occurring at least sixty but not more than one hundred twenty days after its proposal.

Section 2

(a) The Parliament, whenever two-thirds of the members then seated shall deem it necessary, may propose amendments to this Constitution which shall then be included as part of this Constitution on approval by the Prince, occurring at least sixty but not more than one hundred eighty days after its passage by the Parliament. If the Prince does not approve of the amendment, the amendment may be included upon the ratification of the amendment by six sevenths of the people, occurring at least sixty but not more than one hundred twenty days after its passage by the Parliament.

 (b) No amendments to this article shall be passed, unless proposed by the Prince. No amendment shall be passed which restricts the rights of the people as outlined in this constitution. Unless proposed by the Prince, no amendments to Article II.

Section 3.

All amendments must be approved by four fifths of the members of the Grand Council to ensure that they adhere to this article and do not violate the rights of the people.

Molossia
Presidential Proclamations
Proclamation 171016

Changes to National Holidays

His Excellency, The President, after great thought and consideration, has decreed the following changes to our holidays:

Jack Day and Laika Day have been rescinded and Molossia's faithful canines will be celebrated henceforth as the annual Running of the Dogs, AKA La Liberigo, on 26 August or the nearest weekend day before or after.

Mir Day and Tranquility Day are rescinded and Molossia's space accomplishments and those of the world will be celebrated on 4 May (May the Fourth). A rocket or rockets should be launched on or about this day if possible.

Chocolate Mint Day will be celebrated on 19 February, likely in the form of ice cream, as that is The President's favorite flavor.

The annual Spring Jamboree will take place on 22 March.

Molossian Navy Day will be celebrated on 4 June, the date the Navy was created, likely with submarine sandwiches.

Chocolate Chip Cookie Day will be celebrated on 4 August, likely with chocolate cookies, as a nod to Molossia's famed monetary standard.

East Germany Day will be celebrated on 2 November, as the anniversary of our never-ending war with that long-defunct nation.

This Proclamation has the force of law, effective 16 October 2017 XL.

Proclamation 150811

The Meaning of the Name "Molossia"

The name Molossia was chosen at random in 1998 as a replacement for the old name for our nation, Vuldstein. Molossia was chosen without the knowledge that there was an ancient Greek nation named Molossia, which was destroyed by the Romans in 168 BC. When our government was made aware of the original nation of Molossia efforts were made to connect modern Molossia with that nation. For a period of years we promoted a Greek and Greco-Italian aspect to our culture and additionally promoted awareness of ancient Molossia via our website. All that came to a halt in 2002 XXV when we were contacted by some angry Greek journalists and accused of stealing their culture by using the name Molossia. At that time we separated ourselves completely from any connection to the Molossia of ancient Greece and have since explained the origin of our nation's name in other ways. It has been variously described as a adaptation of the Spanish word "morro", meaning rock, and also as a adaptation of the Chinese words for "desert-place-rock" Mň Lů Shí. Neither of these explanations seemed satisfactory, thus it has been decided to establish a new meaning for the name Molossia. After careful consideration, it is determined that henceforth the name Molossia will be known as an adaptation of the Hawaiian word **Maluhia**, which means peace and serenity. While there is no direct connection between Hawaii and Molossia, we have a great admiration for Hawaii and Hawaiian culture, thus this selection of a name origin will bring honor to both our nations.

This Proclamation has the force of law, effective 11 August 2015 XXXXIII.

Proclamation 150223

Farfalla Colony

The Government of the Republic of Molossia proclaims its sovereignty over the Colony of Farfalla, a territory located in central Modoc County, about 11 Imperial Nortons (11 km / 6.5 miles) north of the town of Alturas, California. Farfalla is about

7,965 Square Royal Nortons (2 hectares / 4.9 acres) in area.

The three territories of the Republic of Molossia, Harmony Province, Desert Homestead Province and Farfalla Colony shall be referred to collectively as the Molossian Archipelago.

The three stripes on the Molossian flag shall each stand for one of the territories, blue for Harmony Province, white for Desert Homestead Province and green for Farfalla Colony.

This Proclamation has the force of law, effective 23 February 2015 XXXXIII.

Proclamation 121001

New Laws

The following edicts have been issued by His Excellency, The President:

☐ It is illegal to cause a catastrophe.

☐ Torpedoes may not be set off in the country.

☐ It is illegal to wear cowboy boots unless you already own at least two cows.

☐ Quail have the right of way to cross any street, including driveways.

☐ Sunshine is guaranteed to the masses.

☐ Detonating a nuclear device within the nation will result in a VL 500.- fine.

☐ It is illegal to walk a camel along Alphonse Simms Circle between the hours of 4:00 and 6:00 PM MST.

☐ All persons wishing to keep a rhinoceros as a pet must obtain a VL 100.- license first.

☐ It is illegal to hunt moths under a street light.

☐ Elephants are prohibited from strolling through Red Square unless they are on a leash.

☐ It is illegal to play percussion instruments in any bathroom.

This Proclamation has the force of law, effective 1 October 2012 XXXV.

Proclamation 111124a

Succession

The Government of the Republic of Molossia has recognized Madame Adrianne Baugh, Vice President and First Lady of the Nation as the official successor to His Excellency President Kevin Baugh, President of the Republic of Molossia. Madame Baugh has repeatedly demonstrated her loyalty, devotion and love of Molossia and its people, and none can be considered better to lead the nation in the event of the extended absence, incapacitation or death of The President.

This Proclamation has the force of law, effective 24 November 2011 XXXIV.

Proclamation 111124b

Esperanto

In an effort to advance Molossia's place in the world of nations, and to combat the confusion caused by the myriad of languages spoken worldwide, the Official Second Language of Molossia will be Esperanto. Esperanto has proven itself in over a century of use to be a valuable tool for international communication and understanding. Every effort will be made to promote the language in Molossia and to encourage its use in official as well as personal practices.

This Proclamation has the force of law, effective 24 November 2011 XXXIV.

Proclamation 100209

Internet Access

Inasmuch as information is an essential requirement for individuals to obtain knowledge about their world and to thus make informed decisions regarding matters of a social, political and personal, it is therefore decreed that unrestricted and uncensored access to the internet is a human right for social inclusion. This government will respect and bolster that right in every way possible, to enhance the lives of all Molossian citizens.

This Proclamation has the force of law, effective 9 February 2010 XXXIII.

Proclamation 090106

Plastic Shopping Bags Banned

Inasmuch plastic shopping bags use up natural resources, consume energy to manufacture, create litter, choke marine life and add to landfill waste, plastic bags are henceforth banned in Molossia, and will be replaced with reusable fabric bags exclusively.

This Proclamation has the force of law, effective 6 January 2009 XXXII.

Proclamation 080127

Genocide Denial, et al.

Part I. It is officially illegal to deny, grossly minimize, try to justify or approve of the genocide committed by the German National-Socialist regime during the Second World War.

Part II. It is officially illegal to deny, grossly minimize, try to justify or approve of the genocide of hundreds of thousands to over one and half million Armenians, committed by the Ottoman Empire during the First World War.

Part III. It is officially illegal to deny, grossly minimize, try to justify or approve of the *Holodomor*, the disastrous manifestation of the Soviet famine of 1932-1933 in Ukraine (at the time, the Ukrainian Soviet Socialist Republic, in the Soviet Union), which claimed millions of lives.

This Proclamation has the force of law, effective 27 January 2008 XXXI.

Proclamation 071026

Legal Drinking Age

The legal drinking age in the Republic of Molossia it is the third Tuesday of the second month after the first Spring Equinox that comes at least 1095 days after your 18th birthday, with variations allowed if you were born on the other side of the International Date Line or on Leap Day, unless it was a full moon in which case it's June of the year after.

This Proclamation has the force of law, effective 26 October 2007 XXX.

Proclamation 070625

Annexation of Hawai'i

It is the stance of the Government of the Republic of Molossia that the annexation of the Kingdom of Hawai'i in 1898 was a blatant act of aggression and imperialism on the part of the United States against the Kingdom of Hawai'i. The Government of Molossia furthermore officially condemns "Bayonet Constitution" and overthrow of the Hawai'ian Monarchy by American adventurers and opportunists, and supported by the United States military. We therefore do not recognize the legality of the occupation and annexation of the Hawai'ian Islands by the United States.

This policy, however, resignedly accepts the de facto authority the United States holds over this territory, and does not represent an active desire to oppose such authority in any way at this time.

This Proclamation has the force of law, effective 29 May 2007 XXX.

Proclamation 070326

New Diplomatic Policy

The Republic of Molossia is a sovereign, independent nation. Our nation extends the hand of friendship to all peoples in all lands. We are always interested in exploring positive, informal relations with other countries.

Effective 26 March 2007 XXX the Republic of Molossia will no longer enter into formal diplomatic relations with any other nation. Rather, we will entertain only informal relationships between our nation and others. This change in policy reflects our realization that our foreign policy has been restrictive and not in accordance with the concept of Declarative Statehood. Declarative Statehood is a cornerstone of the concept of small, or micro, nations, and is recognized as canon by certain larger nations, in accordance with the Montevideo Convention of 1933. Simply put, it states that a nation does not have to be recognized by another nation in order for it to exist and be sovereign. This is the approach that Molossia uses to deal with larger nations that do not recognize us (see our policy on Sovereignty). Thus, it is logical to apply the same standard to dealing with smaller, unrecognized nations. Henceforth, our policy is simple, friendship toward other small nations, but no formal relations, to include treaties. They are not necessary; you do not need to to be recognized by Molossia in order to be sovereign, any more than you need to be recognized by a larger nation in order to be sovereign. If you state your sovereignty, that is good enough for our government, as is should be for all.

It is important to understand that this is not an isolationist foreign policy. We welcome friendly informal relations with all nations, large and small, and we pledge our assistance and friendship in helping any new nation develop. Please do not hesitate to contact our government if we can be of any assistance.

This Proclamation has the force of law, effective 26 March 2007 XXX.

Proclamation 070301

Incandescent Light Bulbs Banned

Inasmuch incandescent light bulbs are an inefficient source of illumination, to the extent that 95% of a light bulb's energy is

106

wasted, incandescent bulbs are henceforth banned in Molossia, and will be replaced with fluorescent light bulbs exclusively.

This Proclamation has the force of law, effective 1 March 2007 XXX.

Proclamation 061007

Catfish Banned

Inasmuch as FHM Magazine has snubbed Molossia by bumping a planned article from the November 2006 issue of that magazine and has replaced it with an article about men who catch catfish with their bare hands, catfish and catfish "noodling" are henceforth banned in Molossia.

Bagged Spinach Banned

Inasmuch as bagged spinach from the United States has recently been shown to be contaminated with E.Coli, bagged spinach is now banned in Molossia. Canned spinach is allowed, in deference to the popular influence of Popeye.

This Proclamation has the force of law, effective 7 October 2006 XXIX.

Proclamation 041209

Use of Tobacco Banned

Inasmuch as tobacco use has been repeatedly shown to be dangerous to the health of the user and bystanders, the use of tobacco products is henceforth banned in the Republic of Molossia. Tobacco use will not be allowed anywhere in the nation, in public or in private. Offenders will be fined VL 50. Furthermore, visitors from outside our nation that violate this decree will be expelled.

This Proclamation has the force of law, effective 9 December 2004 XXVII.

Proclamation 031101

Time and Date Policy

Part I.

Molossia as a nation is unique and individual. As such, uniqueness should be fostered in every date. Thus, His Excellency, The President has decreed that Molossia will have its own time zone "Molossian Standard Time". This time zone is to be 19 minutes ahead of Pacific Standard Time and 41 minutes behind Mountain Standard Time. Furthermore, Molossia will not recognize "Daylight Savings Time", and thus clocks will not move forward or back in Molossia. This time will be used for all official functions, and citizens are directed to comply.

Part II.

Henceforth, Molossian dates will be modified. All dates will be written in the standard Gregorian Calendar format, with the addition of a roman numeral afterward. This numeral will reflect the years since the foundation of the Molossian Nation, in 1977. Thus all dates will be written, for example, 30 July 2004 XXVII, "XXVII" indicating 27 years since the foundation of Molossia. This date system will be used for all official functions, and citizens are directed to comply.

This Proclamation has the force of law, effective 1 November 2003 XXVI.

Proclamation 021229a

Environmental Policy

The Government of the Republic of Molossia is committed to protecting and improving the environment in all areas of our nation, by seeking continual improvement of our environment and citizen safety and health. This is part of our commitment to preserve and enhance the environment, safety and health of our citizens and neighbors.

☐ The development and implementation of this policy is a commitment of the Government of the Republic of Molossia and a shared responsibility with our citizens.

☐ The Government of the Republic of Molossia recognizes that a commitment to the following guiding principles is fundamental in carrying out the national environmental policy:

☐ To comply with environmental, safety and health laws and regulations.

☐ To consider environmental impacts as an essential element of life and lifestyle.

☐ To provide and maintain safe and healthy working conditions.

☐ To establish objectives and targets aimed at the prevention of pollution by reducing the generation of waste, recycling waste that is generated, and properly disposing of waste that cannot be recycled.

☐ To encourage conservation of energy, water, and natural resources through increased efficiency and the introduction of new technology.

☐ To provide citizens with a better understanding of environmental issues and the Government's commitment, policies, and programs to preserve and improve the environment.

☐ To openly make this policy available to all citizens. The Government of the Republic of Molossia shall ensure that the environmental policy is clearly understood, implemented, maintained, and communicated throughout the nation. Leaders shall take the environmental policy into consideration in the development of objectives and targets.

This Proclamation has the force of law, effective 29 December 2002 XXV.

────────────────

Proclamation 021229b

Equal Opportunity

The Government of the Republic of Molossia recognizes:

☐ That it exists to serve its citizens.

☐ That its citizens have a diverse range of needs and services will be geared to reflect this. In order to gear services to need and to determine the level of need of its different citizens, it will use a range of methods.

☐ The Government should reflect its citizen's needs at all levels of responsibility.

☐ Those who receive its services are best placed to express an informed view about how things can be done better.

☐ To ensure it is delivering its services in a non-discriminatory way, the Government's performance will be subject to regular monitoring and review.

☐ It will ensure its workforce operates in a non-discriminatory way.

The Government of the Republic of Molossia will:

☐ Take any necessary action to discharge its legal obligations to ensure equality of opportunities and the elimination of unlawful discrimination.

☐ Take action to ensure that equality is at the heart of all Government policies.

☐ Take steps to ensure that all Government employees are aware of the need to operate without discrimination and provide equal opportunities for all disadvantaged groups.

☐ Will promote equal opportunities throughout the nation.

In addition, discrimination against any individual in any manner on the grounds of sexual orientation is absolutely prohibited.

This prohibition extends to the Government of the Republic of Molossia, its agencies, any private organization or agency (to include religious institutions), and any and all private citizens. This prohibition includes but is not limited to: discrimination as regards marriage (Partnering), inheritance, jobs, justice and the redress of wrongs, education, and spiritual sustenance. Verbal discrimination, i.e. disparaging remarks, is equally forbidden.

Furthermore, no distinction will be made between homosexual relationships and heterosexual relationships. Both will be treated equally by the Government of the Republic of Molossia, its agencies, any private organization or agency (to include religious institutions), and any and all private citizens.

This Proclamation has the force of law, effective 29 December 2002 XXV.

Proclamation 020221

Nuclear Free Zone

The United States Government has made and is making repeated efforts to establish a nuclear repository at Yucca Mountain in Southern Nevada. These efforts run in direct opposition to the will of the citizens of the State of Nevada. In addition, these efforts blatantly ignore enormous geological and environmental problems with the chosen repository site. Specifically, the chosen site rests on at least 30 earthquake faults, in an area that demonstrates recent volcanic activity, and has a strong potential for contamination of the aquifer with thallium and uranium leaks from the stored nuclear waste. This aquifer is not localized, but is interconnected with the aquifers of over 70% of the State of Nevada, including that which supplies the Republic of Molossia with its water.

It is the contention of the Government of the Republic of Molossia that the Government of the United States is executing a flawed and dangerous policy in promulgating this site for the long-term storage of nuclear waste. In addition, this government condemns the recent use of the concept of patriotism and "homeland defense" to force this issue on the citizens of Nevada, in defiance of their will. The Government of the Republic of Molossia deplores this project and the shortsighted decision-making that has made this project a reality. It is the opinion of this Government that storing nuclear waste at Yucca Mountain is an extremely bad idea, bordering on criminal.

Effective immediately, the Republic of Molossia is declared a nuclear-free zone. This declaration is made in protest to the United States Government's promulgation of Yucca Mountain as a nuclear repository, and in protest of that government's ignorance of the will of the citizens of this region and of the irreparable environmental damage this project will create.

This Proclamation has the force of law, effective 21 February 2002 XXV.

Proclamation 001014

The U.S.-Mexican War (1846-1848)

It is the stance of the Government of the Republic of Molossia that the U.S.-Mexican War (1846-1848) was a blatant act of aggression and imperialism on the part of the United States against the Mexican Nation. The Government of Molossia officially condemns the invasion and subjugation of the Mexican Nation, and the resultant annexation of 55% percent of its territory. We therefore do not recognise the legality of the occupation of the lands of ceded to the United States after the War, including those now part of the Republic of Molossia.

This policy, however, resignedly accepts the de facto authority the

United States holds over this territory, and does not represent an active desire to oppose such authority in any way at this time.

This Proclamation has the force of law, effective 14 October 2000 XXIII.

Proclamation 001013a

Homosexual Rights

Discrimination against any individual in any manner on the grounds of sexual orientation is absolutely prohibited. This prohibition extends to the Government of the Republic of Molossia, its agencies, any private organization or agency (to include religious institutions), and any and all private citizens. This prohibition includes but is not limited to: discrimination as regards marriage (Partnering), inheritance, jobs, justice and the redress of wrongs, education, and spiritual sustenance. Verbal discrimination, i.e. disparaging remarks, is equally forbidden.

Furthermore, no distinction will be made between homosexual relationships and heterosexual relationships. Both will be treated equally by the Government of the Republic of Molossia, its agencies, any private organization or agency (to include religious institutions), and any and all private citizens.

This Proclamation has the force of law, effective 13 October 2000 XXIII.

Proclamation 001013b

Religion and Political Activity

Religious institutions and the clergy, lay or professional, are prohibited from interfering in, participating in or expressing their views as regards political activities in the Republic of Molossia. This prohibition extends to private conversations between clergy, lay or professional, and the members of their churches, and includes a ban on non-verbal as well as verbal communications.

This Proclamation has the force of law, effective 13 October 2000 XXIII.

Proclamation 001013c

Pregnancy Termination and Assisted Suicide

The Government of the Republic of Molossia considers that the principle of self determination to extends to the individual, beyond that right normally accorded to a people as a group. This personal sovereignty includes the right to make rational decisions regarding an individual's own body, insofar as these decisions do not endanger others (such as wanting to blow oneself up in a crowded square). While this government does not officially condone pregnancy termination, it is forbidden to enact any law or decree restricting a woman's right to select such a method to terminate her pregnancy. This government will not restrict qualified physicians from performing pregnancy termination, nor will it tolerate any actions on the part of individuals or groups to block access to medical facilities performing pregnancy terminations, nor to harass individuals, organizations or medical personnel providing pregnancy termination services.

Furthermore, the Government of the Republic of Molossia extends the right of self determination to those individuals seeking physician-assisted suicide as a recourse to a terminal illness. This Government will not enact any law or decree restricting an individual's right to seek physician-assisted suicide services. This government will not restrict qualified physicians from performing physician-assisted suicide services, nor will it tolerate any actions on the part of individuals or groups to block access to medical facilities performing physician-assisted suicide services, nor to harass individuals, organizations or medical personnel providing physician-assisted suicide services.

This Proclamation has the force of law, effective 13 October 2000 XXIII.

Proclamation 000206

This policy replaces Government Proclamation 990818b, Self-Determination and Diplomatic Recognition

Self-Determination and Diplomatic Recognition

Section A: It is the policy of the Republic of Molossia to support any nation or emerging nation in its quest for self-determination. Freedom, peace and prosperity are overriding goals for most human beings, and all mankind deserves the right to achieve these goals. The Republic of Molossia will therefore support and defend any nation's movement toward independence, and pledges all resources necessary to help their quest for freedom.

Section B: The Republic of Molossia is a sovereign, independent nation. It is not a role playing game (RPG), hobby, nor does it exist solely on the Internet for entertainment purposes. The Republic of Molossia **will not** grant recognition to nor enter into diplomatic relations with any national entity that is purely a hobby, role-playing game, fictitious experiment or exists solely on the Internet or any resemblance thereof. It will, however, accept and consider polite diplomatic overtures addressed to Molossia from other legitimate nations or entities actively pursuing sovereignty and independence, that seek the establishment of mutual recognition and diplomatic relations.

Only those national entities that actively pursue, or state a firm goal of, "real world" sovereignty and independence will be considered for possible recognition by the Republic of Molossia.

Additionally, it is the policy of the Republic of Molossia that an independent nation, or a nation actively seeking independence, will establish and maintain an active Internet presence for a period not less than 90 days, before such nation will be considered for diplomatic recognition.

Furthermore, any request for diplomatic relations will be considered on a case-by-case basis, without exception.

This Proclamation has the force of law, effective 6 February 2000 XXIII.

Proclamation 990903a

Change of the Name of the Molossian Nation

The official title of the Molossian Nation is changed from "The People's Democratic Republic of Molossia" to the "Republic of Molossia".

This Proclamation has the force of law, effective 3 September 1999 XXII.

Proclamation 990903b

Repudiation of Communist Ideology

The Government of Molossia officially renounces Marxism - Leninism as the official and only State Ideology. Henceforth all political philosophies will be equally tolerated in the Republic of Molossia. All Communist symbols will be removed from government institutions, and the Communist Party will cease to be the only authorized political party.

This Proclamation has the force of law, effective 3 September 1999 XXII.

Proclamation 990903c

Declaration of Martial Law

Due to civil unrest, a State of Martial Law is proclaimed for the Republic of Molossia. Henceforth and until further notice, all executive, legislative and judicial powers will be exercised solely by His Excellency, The President. The National Assembly is suspended, public demonstrations are banned and free speech laws are suspended. This ordinance remains in effect indefinitely, and violators are subject to prosecution.

This Proclamation has the force of law, effective 3 September 1999 XXII.

Proclamation 990818a

Residence Conditions for Foreigners and Citizenship Information

Any foreign visitor can stay in Molossia for a period of two weeks as a tourist. A foreign national is not allowed to take up employment or residence without a permit from the Aliens Registration Office and without having registered with this department.

Anyone wishing to stay in Molossia for more than two weeks, or to establish residency or citizenship, must obtain a long-term residence visa. In order to obtain this visa, the individual must apply to the Aliens Registration Office. Long-term residence visas are issued for a maximum period of three months, at which time the individual must either apply for permanent citizenship, or leave the country. Individuals cannot apply for citizenship without first obtaining a long-term residence visa and then waiting for the three month period to expire. During that period of time, the individual may apply and take the citizenship test. Upon successful completion of this test, and the at the expiry of the long-term residence visa, the individual will be issued a Certificate of Citizenship.

Visa and citizenship applications will be handled through the Aliens Registrations Office, Molossian Foreign Ministry.

This Proclamation has the force of law, effective 18 August 1999 XXII.

Proclamation 990818b

Self-Determination and Diplomatic Recognition

Section A: It is the policy of the Republic of Molossia to support any nation or emerging nation in its quest for self-determination. Freedom, peace and prosperity are overriding goals for most human beings, and all mankind deserves the right to achieve these goals. The Republic of Molossia will therefore support and defend any nation's movement toward independence, and pledges all resources necessary to help their quest for freedom.

Section B: The Republic of Molossia will entertain applications for diplomatic recognition from any emerging or extant nation, or any group seeking independence. Territorial sovereignty is not an overriding concern in considering applications for diplomatic recognition. A principal concern, however, is longevity. It has been the experience of this nation that many groups will seek self-determination, and, having achieved some short-term goal other than independence, abandon or lose interest in the cause of independence. Therefore, it is henceforth the policy of the Republic of Molossia that a nation will establish and maintain an active Internet presence for a period not less than 90 days, before such nation will be considered for diplomatic recognition. Exceptions will be granted on a case-by-case basis.

This Proclamation has the force of law, effective 18 August 1999 XXII.

New NeoNebraska
Constitution
Unification Act

Recognizing that these states are different culturally,
Recognizing that these states hold differing interests,

Recognizing that the establishment of a unified republic would end the full sovereignty of the states,
Recognizing that many ideologies must be kept in the republic,

It is hereby the proud declaration of the sovereign state of Hjollkaðr that a union of the lesser republics has been established!

Condition 1
- Each lesser republic will be part of a larger region
- Each region will be composed of exactly five of the lesser republics

Condition 2
- Each region will send three representatives to a Region Legislative Body

Condition 3
-Each lesser republic will send five representatives to a District Legislative Body

Condition 4
- Exactly three leaders will be elected every 5 years, these will be:
1. The Right, Honorable, Lord Governing Executive
2. The State Monarch
3. The People's Premier
- These three will hold the same say in ordinary matters, however the Right, Honorable, Lord Governing Executive will be given control of the military, as well as authority over the economic ties to other nations. They will also be given power to stop all legislative action over a proposal to either legislative body.
- The State monarch will be given full authority over the affairs in the allocated provinces, these being the lesser republics 4, 23, 24, 25, 27, and 28, as well as the overseas territory of the artificial island of the unnamed 31st district.
- The People's premier will be given the privilege of being the ambassador to all international committees, and authority over the domestic and foreign councils.

Condition 5

- The lesser republics will be free to elect to be under the control of the state monarch, and free to decide against it if there is a unanimous vote to exit from the monarch's control.
- Therefore, at any time the people under the control of the monarch are free to split into 6 separate lesser republics.

Condition 6

- All lesser republics to sign are unified under one central government, and are required to participate in democratic elections as well as other state affairs.

Condition 7

- Membership to this union is voluntary, but only reversible with the approval of a majority of votes in both legislative bodies.
- If a lesser republic is seen to be unfit to remain in the union, the republic can be expelled if all three leaders vote to eject it, as well as a majority of votes cast in both legislative bodies
- If a republic is expelled, this means that they are obliged to peacefully surrender the land on which the republic is operating.
- Failure to comply will result in a vote being held to go to war to claim the land.

Acknowledging that you have read this document in its entirety, you hereby pledge unity and service towards the Greater Republic.

Alexei Barthoksson,
Barthok Karffson,
Bjarki Bjarkison,
Dzheimi koks,
Nathaniel dean brother of all that is right and just Hipsherson,
Səmænþə Pitərsson
Seamus Cavanaugh

Reggina
Constitution

The Empire Of Reggina, will, and shall always have:

a desire to establish justice, liberty, and security, and to promote the well-being of all its citizens, and in the exercise of its sovereignty, proclaims its will to:

Guarantee democratic coexistence within the Constitution and the laws, in accordance with a fair economic and social order.

Consolidate a State of Law which ensures the rule of law as the expression of logic, moral, and ethics.

Protect all people of Reggina in the exercise of human rights, culture, traditions, language and institutions.

Promote the progress of culture, and economy to ensure a dignified quality of life for all.

Establish an advanced democratic society, and Cooperate in the strengthening of peaceful relations and effective cooperation among all the peoples of the earth.

Therefore, the Reggina Court pass and people ratify the following **CONSTITUTION**

Preliminary Title:

Section 1

1. Reggina is hereby established as a social and democratic Republic, subject to the rule of law, which advocates freedom, justice, and equality as highest values of its people.

2. National Independence belongs to the Reggina people, from whom all state powers emanate.

3. The political form of Reggina is a Unitary Constitutional Parliamentary Republic with a head Marshall/Prime Minister.

Section 2

The Constitution is based on the indissoluble unity of the Reggina Common Nation, the common and indivisible homeland of all

Reggina People; it recognizes and guarantees the right to self-government of the nationalities and regions of which it is composed and the solidarity among them all.

Section 3

1. English is the official working language of the State. All Reggina Citizens have the duty to know it and the right to use or not use it.

2. The other Roman languages shall also be official in the respective Self-governing Committees in accordance with their Statutes.

3. The richness of the different linguistic modalities of Reggina is a cultural heritage which shall be specially respected and protected.

Section 4

1. The flag of The Empire of Reggina consists of a Reg Background, with a Yellow Bear Tearing apart an atom. Yellow for the community of nations that are allies and under Reggina, Red for the blood spilled in name of Reggina. The Bear represents the never-ending fierceness that drives the citizens of Reggina. The Atom represents that even though the atom is the smallest of matter in the universe, it makes up everything known and unknown to humanity. The Bear tearing apart the Atom represents that We as Reggianans, can and will defend ourselves, no matter the size or number of the foe.

2. The Statutes may recognize flags and ensigns of the Self-governing Communities. These shall be used together with the flag of Reggina on top of said flag on their public buildings and in their official ceremonies.

Section 5

The capital of the State is and always shall be the great city of New Nola

Section 6

Political parties are the expression of political pluralism, they contribute to the formation and expression of the will of the people and are an essential instrument for political participation. Their creation and the exercise of their activities are free in so far as they respect the Constitution and the law. Their internal structure and their functioning must be democratic.

Section 7

Trade unions and employers associations contribute to the defense and promotion of the economic and social interests which they represent. Their creation and the exercise of their activities shall be free in so far as they respect the Constitution and the law. Their internal structure and their functioning must be democratic.

Section 8

1. The mission of the Armed Forces, comprising the Army, the Navy and the Air Force, is to guarantee the sovereignty and independence of Reggina and to defend its territorial integrity and the constitutional order.

2. The basic structure of military organization shall be regulated by an Organic Act in accordance with the principles of the present Constitution.

Section 9

1. Citizens and public authorities are bound by the Constitution and all other legal previsions.

2. It is the responsibility of the public authorities to promote conditions ensuring that freedom and equality of individuals and of the groups to which they belong are real and effective, to remove the obstacles preventing or hindering their full enjoyment, and to facilitate the participation of all citizens in political, economic, cultural and social life.

3. The Constitution guarantees the principle of legality, the hierarchy of legal provisions, the publicity of legal statutes, the non-retroactivity of punitive provisions that are not favorable to or restrictive of individual rights, the certainty that the rule of law shall prevail, the accountability of

public authorities, and the prohibition of arbitrary action of public authorities.

Section 10

1. The dignity of the person, the inviolable rights which are inherent, the free development of the personality, the respect for the law and for the rights of others are the foundation of political order and social peace.

2. Provisions relating to the fundamental rights and liberties recognized by the Constitution shall be construed in conformity with the Universal Declaration of Human Rights and international treaties and agreements thereon ratified by Reggina.

CHAPTER I Federal Citizens and Aliens

Section 11

1. Reggina Citizens nationality shall be acquired, retained and lost in accordance with the provisions of the law.

2. No person of Reggina by birth may be deprived of his or her nationality, unless willfully given up, or in the case of extreme violations of Regginian or international law, in which case, shall always be lost, and will be treated to as an alien, however shall still be treated with given rights. This does affect those with dual citizenship, either by birth or by acquiring.

3. The State may negotiate dual nationality treaties with English speaking countries or with those which have had or which have special links with Reggina. In these countries Reggina citizens may become naturalized without losing their nationality of origin, even if those countries do not grant a reciprocal right to their own citizens.

Section 13

1. Aliens in Reggina shall enjoy the public freedoms guaranteed by the present Part, under the terms to be laid down by treaties and the law.

2. Only Reggina citizens shall have the rights recognized in section 22, except in cases which may be established by treaty or by law concerning

126

the right to vote and the right to be elected in municipal elections, and subject to the principle of reciprocity.

3. Extradition shall be granted only in compliance with a treaty or with the law, on reciprocal basis. No extradition can be granted for political crimes; but acts of terrorism shall not be regarded as such.

4. The law shall lay down the terms under which citizens from other countries and stateless persons may enjoy the right to asylum in Reggins.

CHAPTER II Rights and freedoms

Section 13

1. Reggina Citizens are equal before the law and may not in any way be discriminated against on account of birth, race, sex, religion, opinion or any other personal or social condition or circumstance.

DIVISION 1.ª Fundamental Rights and Public Freedoms

Section 14

Everyone has the right to life and to physical and moral integrity.

Section 15

1. Freedom of ideology, religion and worship of individuals and communities is guaranteed, with no other restriction on their expression than may be necessary to maintain public order as protected by law.

2. No one may be compelled to make statements regarding his or her ideology, religion or beliefs.

3. No religion shall have a state character. The public authorities shall take into account the religious beliefs of Reggina and shall consequently

maintain appropriate cooperation relations with the Catholic Church and other confessions.

Section 16

1. Every person has the right to freedom and security. No one may be deprived of his or her freedom except in accordance with the provisions of this section and in the cases and in the manner provided for by the law.

2. Preventive arrest may last no longer than the time strictly necessary in order to carry out the investigations aimed at establishing the events; in any case the person arrested must be set free or handed over to the judicial authorities within a maximum period of seventy-two hours.

3. Every person arrested must be informed immediately, and in a way understandable to him or her, of his or her rights and of the grounds for his or her arrest, and may not be compelled to make a statement. The arrested person shall be guaranteed the assistance of a lawyer during police and judicial proceedings, under the terms to be laid down by the law.

4. An habeas corpus procedure shall be provided for by law in order to ensure the immediate handing over to the judicial authorities of any person illegally arrested. Likewise, the maximum period of provisional imprisonment shall be determined by law and/or times of war.

5) Under circumstances torture shall be used in certain times to receive information against and enemy nation, while at war. This will never be used on a Reggina citizen, unless that said citizen is a proven guilty of terrorism, or is proved guilty of treason. The death penalty is and will be used always for treason, terrorism, and in times where the judicial process grants the crime fit to apply.

Section 17

1. The right to honor, to personal and family privacy and to the own image is guaranteed.

2. The home is inviolable. No entry or search may be made without the consent of the householder or a legal warrant except in the case of flagrant unlawful actions.

3. Secrecy of communications is guaranteed, particularly regarding postal, telegraphic and telephonic communications, except in the event of a court order.

4. The law shall restrict the use of data processing in order to guarantee the honor and personal and family privacy of citizens and the full exercise of their rights.

Section 18

Reggina citizens have the right to freely choose their place of residence, and to freely move about within the national territory. Likewise, they have the right to freely enter and leave Reggina subject to the conditions to be laid down by the law and/or times of war. This right may not be restricted for political or ideological reasons

Section 19

1. The following rights are recognized and protected:

a) The right to freely express and spread thoughts, ideas and opinions through words, in writing or by any other means of reproduction. Unless said information is considered secret by the Federal leadership.

b) The right to literary, artistic, scientific and technical production and creation.

c) The right to academic freedom.

d) The right to freely communicate or receive truthful information by any means of dissemination whatsoever. The law shall regulate the right to the clause of conscience and professional secrecy in the exercise of these freedoms.

e) The right to bear arms

2. The exercise of these rights may not be restricted by any form of prior censorship.

3. The law shall regulate the organization and parliamentary control of the mass-communication means under the control of the State or any public agency and shall guarantee access to such means by the significant social and political groups, respecting the pluralism of society and of the various languages of Reggina.

4. These freedoms are limited by respect for the rights recognized in this Part, by the legal provisions implementing it, and especially by the right to honor, to privacy, to the own image and to the protection of youth and childhood.

5. The seizure of publications, recordings and other means of information may only be carried out by means of a court order.

Section 20

1. The right to peaceful unarmed assembly is granted. The exercise of this right shall not require prior authorization.

2. In the case of meetings in public places and of demonstrations, prior notification shall be given to the authorities, who can only forbid them when there are well founded grounds to expect a breach of public order, involving danger to persons or property.

Section 21

1. The right of association is granted.

2. Associations which pursue ends or use means legally defined as criminal offenses are illegal.

3. Associations set up on the basis of this section must be entered in a register for the sole purpose of public knowledge.

4. Associations may only be dissolved or have their activities suspended by virtue of a court order stating the reasons for it.

Section 22

1. Citizens have the right to participate in public affairs, directly or through representatives freely elected in periodic elections by universal suffrage.

2. They also have the right to accede under conditions of equality to public functions and positions, in accordance with the requirements laid down by the law.

Section 23

1. All persons have the right to obtain effective protection from the judges and the courts in the exercise of their rights and legitimate interests, and in no case may there be a lack of defense.

2. Likewise, all have the right to the ordinary judge predetermined by law; to defense and assistance by a lawyer; to be informed of the charges brought against them; to a public trial without undue delays and with full guarantees; to the use of evidence appropriate to their defense; not to make self-incriminating statements; not to plead themselves guilty; and to be presumed innocent.

The law shall specify the cases in which, for reasons of family relationship or professional secrecy, it shall not be compulsory to make statements regarding allegedly criminal offenses.

Section 24

1. No one may be convicted or sentenced for actions or omissions which when committed did not constitute a criminal offense, misdemeanor or administrative offense under the law then in force.

2. The Civil Administration may not impose penalties which directly of indirectly imply deprivation of freedom.

Section 25

Courts of Honor are prohibited within the framework of the Civil Administration and of professional organizations.

Section 26

1. Everyone has the right to education. Freedom of teaching is recognized.

2. Education shall aim at the full development of human personality with due respect for the democratic principles of coexistence and for basic rights and freedoms.

3. The public authorities guarantee the right of parents to ensure that their children receive religious and moral instruction in accordance with their own convictions.

4. Elementary education is compulsory and free. Unless said school is privately owned.

5. The public authorities guarantee the right of all to education, through general education programming, with the effective participation of all sectors concerned and the setting-up of educational centres.

6. The right of individuals and legal entities to set up educational centres is recognized, provided they respect constitutional principles.

7. Teachers, parents and, when appropriate, pupils shall participate in the control and management of all centres supported by the Administration out of public funds, under the terms established by the law.

8. The public authorities shall inspect and standardize the educational system in order to ensure compliance with the laws.

9. The public authorities shall help the educational centres which meet the requirements established by the law.

10. The autonomy of Universities is recognized, under the terms established by the law.

Section 27

1. All have the right to freely join a trade union. The law may restrict or except the exercise of this right in the Armed Forces or Institutes or other bodies subject to military discipline, and shall lay down the special conditions of its exercise by civil servants. Trade union freedom includes the right to set up trade unions and to join the union of one's choice, as well as the right of trade unions to form confederations and to found

international trade union organizations, or to become members thereof. No one may be compelled to join a trade union.

2. The right of workers to strike in defense of their interests is recognized. The law governing the exercise of this right shall establish the safeguards necessary to ensure the maintenance of essential public services.

3. However if said unions are founded without the notification of the company, and the state Committee that of which the workers are working thereof, then members of said union, shall be fined up to $200, (which will be adjusted to inflation, and economy), and/or fired, and/ or work up to 24 hours community service.

Section 28

1. All Reggina citizens shall have the right to individual and collective petition, in writing, in the manner and subject to the consequences to be laid down by law.

2. Members of the Armed Forces or Institutes or bodies subject to military discipline may only exercise this right individually and in accordance with statutory provisions relating to them.

Sealand
Constitution[9]

Preliminary Remark

Sealand is an island in the southern part of the North Sea, Latitude 51-53 North, Longitude 01-28 East. The Principality of Sealand was founded in 1967 and founded as a sovereign state. The

[9] This version of the Sealand Constitution is as originally signed in 1976, available here as part of the creative commons **CC BY-SA 3.0** license, as written by Paddy Roy Bates. License: https://creativecommons.org/licenses/by-sa/3.0/legalcode. Source: https://en.wikisource.org/wiki/Constitution_of_the_Principality_of_Sealand

Sovereign of the Principality of Sealand H. H. Prince Roy of Sealand has proclaimed in 1975 a fundamental law to his state. Based on this constitution several laws become legal. The Knowledge of present laws is fundamentally important for national and international relations.

This first publication of the gather statutes gives also information of special laws, but they do not cancel the British Law of Contract and the British Common Law on which the law of the Principality of Sealand is a modern state of Justice.

- May 1976, Roy of Sealand.

Preamble

In consciousness of his responsibility before God and before man, and inspired by the will to serve the cause of Peace for his People and for all peoples in the world, the sovereign ruler of the Principality of Sealand, His majesty Prince Roy of Sealand, for himself and for his successors to the throne, by virtue of his constitutional authority resolves, swears and proclaims the following.

Section 1

1.1. The dignity of man is unimpeachable. To respect and preserve this dignity is the duty of all national authority. **1.2** The Sovereign and his people acknowledge the inviolable and inalienable rights of man as the basis of every human community, of freedom and of justice in the world, and recognize that these rights are in complete accord with the General Declaration of Human Rights as already defined by other States on December 10th, 1948. **1.3** The following rights are binding on the Sovereign, his successors, the legislature, the executive authority and the administration of justice, as immediately effective by the law.

Section 2

2.1 Everyone has the right to the free development of his or her personality, as far as this does not infringe upon the rights of others. **2.2** Everyone has the right to life and physical safety. The freedom of the person is unassailable and may be restricted only by law.

Section 3

All men are equal before the law. No one may suffer prejudice because of his or her sex, descent, race, language, native land and extraction, his or her faith or religious convictions.

Section 4

4.1 A subject of the State is that person who possesses citizenship or acquires it. **4.2** The first citizen is the Sovereign. All executive power originates from him. This supreme power is passed on to the Sovereign's heir, who is designated by him. The Sovereign designates this heir on the proclamation of this law, later upon taking over supreme power, and also designates at least the next two in line of succession. Should certain heirs or next in line of succession not be able to accept the supreme power because they have died, and should further heirs not have been appointed, the Privy Council decides upon a person as Sovereign. In the case of equal voting, the President of the Privy Council has the casting vote. **4.3** Members of the Privy Council, those entrusted with political assignments, members of the government, chargè d'affaires and members of the diplomatic service are always citizens of the State by reason of thend their citizenship. **4.4** Other persons acquire nationality by conferring of this by the Sovereign. An appointed consul will be given preference when laying claim to citizenship. **4.5** Legal persons and corporations who prove their domicile by registration in a register especially furnished by law for the purpose are citizens. **4.6** No citizen may be extradited at the demand of another state unless authorized by the Sovereign. **4.7** A dispossession of nationality is only permissible when as a result the person concerned does not become stateless, except where the Sovereign considers that it is necessary for such dispossession in the best interest of SEALAND or any of its citizens.

Section 5

Should for any cause or by reason of any law whatsoever, the State be transferred to another, be united with another state, or be changed into a federation, or be changed for any other reasons of whatever kind, the nationality of SEALAND continues to be valid until the possessor of its citizenship accepts the citizenship of another nation.

Section 6

6.1 The ministers of the country, the President of the High Court, the President of the STATE BANK, and two further persons called upon by the Sovereign constitute the Privy Council, which is bound under obligation to advise the Sovereign. The Minister of Foreign Affairs is the President of the Privy Council. **6.2** A member of the Privy Council may not be called to account for a punishable offence, unless the Sovereign, expressly authorizes the commencement of proceedings.

Section 7

7.1 All citizens have the right to choose their profession freely. No one may be forced to do a certain work. **7.2** The practicing of a profession may be regulated by law.

Section 8

8.1 All citizens enjoy freedom of movement within all territories of the State. **8.2** This right may be limited by law only when sufficient means for supporting life are not available, or when special burdens would ensue for the State, or in cases where it is necessary to prevent access for reasons of national security, for control of epidemics, natural catastrophes or especially severe disasters, or if it is necessary to prevent punishable actions, or actions which the Sovereign and Privy Council consider are likely to lead to such actions. **8.3** SEALAND will not provide a haven for any person who is fleeing from justice.

Section 9

9.1 The safety of the houses, property and the right of inheritance of all citizens will be respected by SEALAND. **9.2** The same limitations as in Section 8.2 are here valid.

Section 10

10.1 section 10.1. Whoever as a citizen misuses the fundamental regulations of the State forfeits his or her fundamental rights. **10.2** Insofar an only a restriction of the basic regulations of the State is foreseen in this law, the appropriate law must be valid in general and not for the individual case.

Section 11

11.1 The legislature is bound to constitutional order, the executive authority and legal decisions in law and justice. **11.2** All state nationals have the right to resist anyone who attempts to set aside this regulation, if other redress is not possible.

Section 12

12.1 All legislation rests with the Sovereign. **12.2** For the preservation of peace and for security of the country, the Sovereign may by law consent to the restriction of the Sovereign's power. **12.3** For the settlement of international disputes the Sovereign assents to entering into agreements concerning a general comprehensive, obligatory, international jurisdiction of arbitration. **12.4** The Legal system, otherwise, is based on the British Common Law and the British Law of Contract. This does not exclude certain special laws which then take precedence over this law. **12.5**

- The Sovereign especially exercises the exclusive jurisdiction over taxes, customs duties, privileges and monopolies.

- Revenues from these laws belong to the Sovereign as well as to the ministries or the representatives of monopolies, in accordance with contractually regulated ratio of distribution. Changes in legally stipulated taxes or privileges can be made only with the agreement of the person concerned or at reasonable interval of time.

- The levying of customs duties and taxes is made by the Ministry of Finances, on the advice of the Privy Council.

- The Sovereign takes the necessary steps to ensure that an audit of accounts and an examination of the ratio of distribution takes place.

Section 13

The general provisions of international law are a constituent part of the constitutional law of SEALAND and have precedence over other laws; they create rights and duties directly for the nationals of the State.

Section 14

The national flag is rectangular, red in the upper diagonal half and black in the lower diagonal half, save that a white diagonal bar forms part of such lower diagonal part of the flag.

Section 15

The national language is English.

Section 16

All the merchant ships of the State form a centralized merchant fleet.

Section 17

For maintenance of order and security the State may legally raise a body of police, with the approval of the Sovereign or the competent Ministry, employ them for this purpose.

Section 18

18.1 For the maintenance of law and order there is the national Tribunal, divided into two senates, the first senate is responsible for matter of international law, public law and constitutional law;

the second senate is responsible for all other legal matters. **18.2** Each senate has a president. The president of the first senate is the President of the Supreme Court of Justice and member of the Privy Council. **18.3** The second senate is the Court of Appeal for the Boards of Justice subordinate to it. **18.4** At least two persons are appointed to each senate, and at least one person to each Board of Justice, and they must establish their qualification for juridical function. **18.5** The courts work out their regulations of procedure themselves, within the framework of this law.

Section 19

19.1 Everyone may claim to be legally heard before the Court. **19.2** A person can only be sentenced when the offence was legally defined before the deed was committed. No criminal act will be retrospectively made such an offence. **19.3** No one may be convicted more than once for the same offence. **19.4** There is no death sentence. **19.5** Imprisonment is permitted only with the approval of the President of the Supreme Court, or his authorized deputy. **19.6** The right of granting a pardon is a prerogative of the Sovereign.

Section 20

20.1 The Sovereign appoints the President of the National State Bank, who is entrusted with carrying out of everything connected with putting into circulation of money, the provision of loans, the security of the currency and the handling of the clearing system at home and abroad. **20.2** The right to the minting of money is not a matter for the State Bank which, however, must be informed of the monetary circulation. **20.3** The legal currency is the SEALAND Dollar. All the services of the State and organs of the State should be settled preferably in this currency. **20.4** Penal provisions for the money and coinage can be legally regulated only with the agreement of the Sovereign.

Section 21

21.1 The Sovereign fills all necessary Ministries with ministers by appointment. **21.2** Necessary Ministries are:

- the Foreign Office,

- the Ministry of Justice,

- the Ministry for Economics and Finances,

- the Ministry for Home Affairs and Development,

- the Ministry for Traffic, Transport, Post and Cultural Affairs,

- the Special Ministry for all other national and international matters,

- and such other Ministries as the Sovereign may from time to time decide.

21.3 Each Ministry equips itself with its own organisation. **21.4** It is permissible for a minister to serve in various ministries. **21.5** Drafts of laws for a Ministry are to be justified in detail to the Sovereign. **21.6** Laws promulgated by the Sovereign are to be published in a National Memorandum.

Section 22

22.1 For special services for the State, the Sovereign awards orders, titles and privileges. **22.2** The Honours listed in section 22.1 will be created by the Sovereign by special law, and the rights conferred by these Honours documented. **22.3** Orders, titles and privileges can also be awarded as hereditary orders, titles and privileges. **22.4** The Privy Council can put forward to the Sovereign the names of suitable persons on whom Honours may be bestowed.

Section 23

23.1 This law comes into force on the day on which the Sovereign signs it. **23.2** All institutions and organs of the State are to be sworn in at the Constitution. By his signature the Sovereign confirm this Constitution by affirmation under oath.

Tax Law

Sec. 1

The PRINCIPALITY OF SEALAND imposes taxes under this law.

Sec. 2

Taxes are non-recurring and are imposed by the PRINCIPALITY OF SEALAND. Fees for the maintenance of the administration are not taxes.

Sec. 3

This Tax Law is valid in the Sovereign territory of the PRINCIPALITY OF SEALAND.

Sec. 4

In certain special cases by special regulation of the Sovereign it may be ordered that no taxes shall be imposed, for example, if only small amounts of tax would result or, if assessment of taxes and imposition of taxes would be inequitable or an undue hardship under the circumstances of individual case but the decision shall always be that of the Sovereign or his duly authorized representative.

Sec. 5

The information contained in all tax returns made by taxpayers will not be disclosed to anybody other than the State of SEALAND and its representatives.

Sec. 6

For the assessment, imposition, and review of all taxes the State of SEALAND or an office or person designated by it will have jurisdiction.

Sec. 7

Terms for the presentation of tax returns or payments may be prolonged by the State of SEALAND or its representative.

Sec. 8

Any decision relating to the tax assessed or waived will be communicated to the taxpayer by the State. A tax receipt will be given for all tax payments. All decisions made against the taxpayer may be revoked by the State in favor of the taxpayer.

Sec. 9

A taxpayer is a person who has to pay taxes under the Tax Law of the State.

Sec. 10

There may be granted a respite in payment of taxes by the State but if it thinks it necessary to make the taxpayer enter into a conditional bail bond either with or without a surety it shall have the power to do so.

Sec. 11

Tax statutes become barred after two years. The barring begins the 31st of December of each year. A demand for such taxes prevents the bar from operating and this shall be so whether the demand is actually received by the taxpayer or not as the posting of a demand by the State or its authorized representative shall be considered sufficient demand in this connection.

Sec. 12

Regarding the statutory obligation to keep books and make out balance sheets and profit and loss accounts, the regulations of other laws are valid also for the fiscal law.

Sec. 13

Tax returns of companies have to be presented in a term of eight months after the end of a calendar year. Natural persons have to present tax returns during the same time virtue of this requirement.

Sec. 14

Declarations of value in the tax returns have to be made in the National currency (SEALAND Dollar).

Sec. 15

The STATE OF SEALAND or an office or person designated by it, shall assist the taxpayer in establishing correct tax returns.

Sec. 16

The taxpayer has to permit the fiscal authorities to inspect all books and records and to be informed of all relevant matters relating to profits and in situ. Hereunder falls also the audit of books.

Sec. 17

The fiscal authority of the State is entitled to enforce the adherence to the regulations and in the event of default by the taxpayer the State may make a penal assessment on the taxpayer which he will then pay.

Sec. 18

The taxpayer is entitled to protest against a tax assessment before the competent court of the PRINCIPALITY OF SEALAND. This relief sought has to be made within a term of three months after posting of the assessment.

Sec. 19

The failure to comply with the tax law and the nonpayment of taxes entitles the State of SEALAND to seize and sell the assets of the taxpayer, but only to the amount of the debited taxes and the expenses of recovering the same.

Sec. 20

Natural persons are liable to an income-tax on all incomes earned in Sealand. Artificial persons like corporate entities and companies also are subject to income-tax. Income is profit out of industrial activity, profit out of capital assets, and profit out of leasing activities.

Sec. 21

Income-tax will normally be at the rate of thirty percent of the income.

Sec. 22

Profit is the increase of assets during one year subject to addition and subtraction of investments and withdrawals and such allowances as may from time to time be permitted by the State. Expenses which do not operate for the maintenance, obtaining, and securing of profit have to be disregarded in assessing profits.

Sec. 22.1

Depreciation for wearing out of assets of a wasting nature is permitted in a reasonable form.

Sec. 23

Natural persons are entitled to a special income-tax exemption. They are not liable to tax on incomes up to an amount of SEALAND Dollar 5,000.

With more than SEALAND Dollar 9,001 they are liable to full income-tax on any excess over this figure.

Sec. 24

Capital profits for example from the sale of shares, business interests, firms, etc. are not normally liable to taxes.

Sec. 25

Assets situated in the PRINCIPALITY OF SEALAND are liable to property tax and death duty. There are not imposed any property taxes or death duties at the moment. Nevertheless the State is entitled to impose those taxes, subject to announcement two years in advance.

Sec. 26

The State is entitled to make administrative regulations subject to ratification by the Sovereign.

Sec. 27

This law comes into force the day this document is signed by the Sovereign.

- 17th May 1976, Roy of Sealand

Law concerning the STATE BANK OF THE PRINCIPALITY OF SEALAND

With reference to section 20 of the Constitution, the following law is published on October 1st, 1975, for the STATE BANK OF SEALAND:

Sec. 1

The STATE BANK shall bear the designation "STATE BANK OF THE PRINCIPALITY OF SEALAND"

Sec. 2

The State Bank is a direct legal person of the PRINCIPALITY OF SEALAND and has its domicile in SEALAND with the right to operate branches and appoint agents in any part of the world.

Sec. 3

The STATE BANK, with the help of powers concerning Currency policy which are vested in the State Bank by law, shall regulate the money circulation and the credit supply of the PRINCIPALITY with the aim of safeguarding the currency and banking side of payment transactions at home and abroad.

Sec. 4

The STATE BANK shall be managed by the President of the STATE BANK. He is responsible for executing decrees issued by the State Council on the subject of money and currency.

Sec. 4.1

The President of the STATE BANK shall be appointed by the Sovereign.

Sec. 4.2

The President of the STATE BANK must have special professional qualifications and be approved by the Privy Council from time to time.

Sec. 4.3

The President of the STATE BANK has the right to carry out:

Sec. 4.4

Foreign exchange transactions and business abroad;

Sec. 4.5

Dealings on the open market;

Sec. 4.6

Looking after central duties for safeguarding the currency and issue of banknotes; and

Sec. 4.7

Deposit and investment.

Sec. 5

The President of the STATE BANK must inform and advise the Sovereign and the State Council in matters of importance with regard to currency policy.

Sec. 6

The STATE BANK has the exclusive right to issue banknotes. These notes are made out in SEALAND Dollars and are the only unrestricted paper legal tender. The smallest banknote is for fifty SEALAND Dollars. The STATE BANK may withdraw banknotes from circulation. The STATE BANK is not obliged to replace notes which have become lost, destroyed, forged, counterfeit or invalid.

Sec. 7

The STATE BANK shall fix the interest rates and, when the case arises, discount rates to be used in each case for its transactions for the purpose of controlling money circulation and borrowing and shall define the principles for its credit business and open market operations.

Sec. 8

Banks domiciled in SEALAND and wishing to conduct business need the authorization of the STATE BANK. When granting this permit, the State Bank may impose restrictions. Observance of these restrictions shall be controlled by the State Bank or by an inspection organization appointed by it. Violations may be punished by withdrawal of the permit to operate a bank.

Sec. 9

The State Bank must advise on the issue of coins. It does not have the right to mint coins itself. Have them minted, or to put them into circulation in some other way.

Sec. 10

The State Bank may transact business with natural and legal persons, authorities or other institutions of a kind either at home or abroad. Business transactions in this sense are:

Sec. 10.1

buying and selling of bills of exchange and cheques foreign currency

Sec. 10.2

buying and selling of debts and securities as well gold, silver and platinum

Sec. 10.3

granting of loans against securities

Sec. 10.4

taking charge or custody of valuables and securities

Sec. 10.5

accepting cheques, bills, money, orders, securities and interest coupons for collection

Sec. 10.6

carrying out other banking commissions and business

Sec. 11

The State Bank's financial year is the calendar year. An annual account made out in SEALAND dollars must be produced and shall be examined at the request of the Sovereign.

Sec. 12

The net profit is to be used as follows:

Sec. 12.1

10% of the net profit is to be used as reserve fund

Sec. 12.2

20% of the net profit is to be carried to a special revenue fund

Sec. 12.3

the rest is to be paid over to the PRINCIPALITY or as otherwise decided by the Privy Council

Sec. 13

The annual account of the STATE BANK shall be published at the request of the Sovereign and shall show:

Sec. 13.1

Assets: gold, silver, platinum, credit at banks, foreign currency and cheques, bills of exchange accounts receivable

Sec. 13.2

Registering regulations etc. do not apply to the STATE BANK. The President of the STATE BANK shall be entered in the commissioned register of the PRINCIPAL OF SEALAND.

Sec. 14

Any person distributing money tokens (coins, notes) or using them for payment without authorization shall be punished. In addition all international regulations on fraud and attempted fraud will apply.

Sec. 15

The President of the State Bank shall organize the State Bank as his own responsibility.

- Roy of Sealand

Law relating to the keeping of registers in the field of powers of Attorney, Registration of companies and shipping

Sec. 1

All persons and institutions entrusted with activities under public law by the Sovereign of the PRINCIPALITY OF SEALAND have to be recorded in a special register, whereby the extent of the authorization has to be specified in detail. All persons and institutions will be recorded in the same register of Powers of Attorney (Register A) with detailed specification of the authorization, who are authorized for a natural or an artificial person of the PRINCIPALITY OF SEALAND.

Sec. 2

All Companies having limited liability and Corporations will be recorded in the public Register of Companies (Register B). Only such registered companies and corporations are considered as having their domicile in the PRINCIPALITY OF SEALAND.

Sec. 3

The minimum issued share capital of a private limited liability company is SEALAND Dollar 40,000.

Sec. 4

All companies incorporated in Register B have to deposit with the STATE BANK of SEALAND a sum equal to 10 % of its issued capital. This deposit will earn interest at the rate of 4 % per annum and will be refunded to the Company or its liquidator upon dissolution but such money will be available for creditors (if any) on such dissolution.

Sec. 5

Before any company can be incorporated in the PRINCIPALITY OF SEALAND it is neccessary for it to register in Register B, and founders to satisfy the Registrar of Companies as to its articles of association, and that it owns the designated capital, and to prove its compliance with § 4 of this law.

Sec. 6

The Registrar of Companies or such person as may be authorized by him from time to time shall have the right to audit and examine the balance sheet and profit and loss account of the company and its Directors shall not later than 8 months after the end of each year, of each company file with the Registrar a statement of the business status and business activity, and of the assets of such company and also a balance sheet and profit and loss account and such accounts shall form the basis of assessment of the companies taxes.

Sec. 7

If any company registered in Register B fails to file its balance sheet and profit and loss account within eight months of its due date, or if the company becomes insolvent and does not pay its debts or its taxes, or if for any other reason the Registrar of Companies is of the opinion that it is just and equitable that the company should be dissolved, he shall have the right so to dissolve the company and appoint a liquidator to collect in the company's assets and pay its debts in such priority as may from time to time apply to SEALAND companies. But so that all moneys due to the State of SEALAND shall be paid in priority to all other debts. Any surplus after paying all costs and expenses of liquidation will be refunded to the share holders in the company.

Sec. 8

On request of the audit company, persons registered in Register B have to insure their material assets with an Insurance Company of SEALAND founded for this reason.

Sec. 9

This law comes into force the day this document is signed by the Sovereign.

- 17th May 1976, Roy of Sealand

Laws relating to passports and visas

Sec. 1

Sealanders and foreigners who enter or leave the territory of the PRINCIPALITY OF SEALAND are obliged to prove their identity by a valid passport and on entering to have a visa entered in such passport.

Sec. 2

In special cases the Sovereign may declare that there will be granted special or general exemption from the obligation to carry a passport or visa.

Sec. 3

Only SEALAND Nationals may receive a passport of the PRINCIPALITY OF SEALAND, although in special cases the Sovereign has the right to issue a passport to a person who is not a National.

Sec. 4

In cases where the Sovereign considers it might endanger the interests of the PRINCIPALITY OF SEALAND to issue a passport to any person or to permit a person to whom a passport has been issued to retain it, such passport may be refused or withdrawn.

Sec. 5

The Sovereign or such person as may from time to time be designated by him will be responsible for the issue of passports and visas.

Sec. 6

All issues or withdrawings of passports as well as all visas will be recorded in a register.

Sec. 7

Fees and expenses have to be paid in national currency (SEALAND Dollar) to the office issuing the passport or visa.

Sec. 8

This law comes into force the day this document is signed by the Sovereign.

- 17th May 1976, Roy of Sealand

Consular Laws

Sec. 1

Consular officials (professional consular officials and consular officials by title) are appointed

Sec. 1.1

to assist in the cooperation between the PRINCIPALITY OF SEALAND and the host countries,

Sec. 1.2

to offer Sealanders as well as artificial Sealandic persons advice and assistance.

Sec. 2

In performance of their duties, the consular officials have to protect and promote the prestige and interests of the PRINCIPALITY OF SEALAND.

Sec. 3

In legal matters, consular officials shall make use of the advice and assistance of a person of their confidence, resident in the host country while performing their duties (usually a person authorized by the law of the host country to give professional legal Advice.)

Sec. 4

The consular officials shall perform duties and rights conferred on them by special regulations, while taking over the consular activity. These may be:

Sec. 4.1

matters of Nationality,

Sec. 4.2

matters of passports and visa,

Sec. 4.3

matters of shipping,

Sec. 4.4

legal matters,

Sec. 4.5

serservices,

Sec. 4.6

supervision of contracts,

Sec. 4.7

assistance to Sealanders,

Sec. 4.8

assistance in cases of disasters,

Sec. 4.9

assistance to Sealandic prisoners on trial and convicts,

Sec. 4.10

acceptance of declarations for use in SEALAND,

Sec. 4.11

legalization of foreign documents,

Sec. 4.12

legalizations in general.

Sec. 5

Professional consular officials are members of the Foreign Ministry of the PRINCIPALITY OF SEALAND and always nationals.

Sec. 6

Consuls by title are honorary officials who are entrusted with the performance of consular duties. They may be Sealanders as well as foreigners.

Sec. 7

The authorization to perform consular duties may be restricted or cancelled at any time. Claims for compensation for consular officials may be directed to the Foreign Ministry but there does not exist a legal claim to the receipt of any fees or compensation and all fees received by any consular official from a third party are the property of SEALAND.

Sec. 8

All consular officials have to be recorded in a register established for this purpose.

Sec. 9

This law comes into force the day this document is signed by the Sovereign.

17th May May 1976, Roy of Sealand

Law referring to the Award of the ORDER OF SEALAND

Sec. 1

For services of special merit to the PRINCIPALITY OF SEALAND the Sovereign of the PRINCIPALITY OF SEALAND hereby donates the ORDER OF SEALAND in order to visibly express appreciation and acknowledgment.

Sec. 2

The ORDER OF SEALAND is awarded as

Sec. 2.1

The GRAND ORDER OF SEALAND

Sec. 2.2

The DISTINGUISHED ORDER OF SEALAND

Sec. 2.3.

The ORDER OF SEALAND, First Class

Sec. 2.4.

The ORDER OF SEALAND, Second Class

Sec. 3

The medal symbol is a red lined cross of white enamel, the joists of which are tapered. In the centre are placed the State arms on a black background. The Grand ORDER OF SEALAND wears underneath the shield two crossed golden swords. The ribbon of the order is red with a white-black border.

Sec. 4

Form and mode of wearing of the ORDER OF SEALAND:

Sec. 4.1

The GRAND ORDER OF SEALAND is worn around the neck on a red ribbon. Additionally there is worn a ribbon from the right shoulder towards the left hip. The ribbon is red. Together with the GRAND ORDER OF SEALAND there is worn an octagonal golden star on the left chest, the centre of which bears the State arms.

Sec. 4.2

The DISTINGUISHED ORDER OF SEALAND is worn according to § 4, sub-section 1, on a red ribbon. There belongs to it the same shoulder-ribbon as under § 4, sub- section 1. Together with it is worn a golden star as under § 4, sub-section 1 but hexagonal.

Sec. 4.3

The ORDER OF SEALAND, first class, is worn on a ribbon at the left chest.

Sec. 4.4

The ORDER OF SEALAND, second class, is worn on a small ribbon at the left upper chest.

Sec. 4.5

All owners of the ORDER OF SEALAND are entitled to wear the corresponding rosette. The joint wearing of order and rosette is not permissible.

Sec. 5

The award of the order is made by the Sovereign. The award is recorded in a Special Order Register. The recipient receives a certificate of the award as well as the order which will be his own property.

Sec. 6

The Sovereign is entitled to revoke the authorization of wearing the Order of SEALAND if he considers that the holder at anytime becomes unworthy.

Sec. 7

The foundation of the order and its conditions will come into force the day this document is signed by the Sovereign.

- 17th May 1976, Roy of Sealand

Seborga[10]

Constitution[11]

CONSTITUTION OF THE PRINCIPALITY OF SEBORGA

TITLE I. - PRINCIPALITY - PUBLIC AUTHORITIES

Art. 1. - The Principality of Seborga is a Sovereign and Independent State within the framework of the general principles of international law.

The territory of the Principality of Seborga is inalienable.

Art. 1-1. - The Principality of Seborga is not part of the Italian State, no longer depends on its Administration, and therefore, the Principality of Seborga is endowed with its Central Electronic Public Administration and its own Hotel de la Prévôté.

Art. 1-2. - The Principality of Seborga recognizes the Republic of Italy as being outside its territory.

Art. 1-3. - The Principality of Seborga conducts its business and financial operations in tax free zone.

Art. 1-4. - Administrative formalities relating to the registration of associations as well as commercial structures are directly managed by an authorized body of the Principality.

Art. 1-5. - The Central Bank of the Principality of Seborga (BCPS) is the only authority to issue approvals to financial institutions wishing to locate in its territory.

---

[10] Seborga, as a functioning region of Italy that proclaims itself a principality, has extensive civil and criminal codes and rules of procedure. These are, however, in Italian, and were they not would still take up too great a proportion of this volume to warrant complete inclusion.

[11] The following is as automatically translated to English from Italian

Art. 1-6. - The Principality of Seborga claims its access to the sea according to the cadastre, its port, its maritime territory as well as its territorial waters.

Art. 2. - The Principality of Seborga declares to be Neutral.

Art. 3. - The Principality applies the Vienna Conventions on Diplomatic and Consular Relations of 1961 and 1963.

Art. 4. - The principle of government is the constitutional monarchy.
The Principality is a State of law committed to respect for fundamental rights and freedoms.

Art. 5. - The executive and legislative powers are exercised by the Chancellor, Ministers, Secretaries of State, High Dignitaries of the State, by the Council of the Crown and the Sovereign Council.

Art. 6. - The judicial power is exercised by the courts and tribunals.

Art. 7. - The separation of administrative, legislative and judicial functions is ensured.

Art. 8. - The coat of arms of the Principality of Seborga is a rose of gold placed on a cross pattée and alaisée Azure on bottom of silver. The shield resting on a mantle Gules, lined with gold, lined with ermine and summoned by a closed crown of gold. Currency: Sub Umbra Sedi.
Historical research is underway to determine if there are older Coats of Arms than currently used.

Art. 8-1. - The Flag of the Principality of Seborga consists of a support gironné and sliced silver and azure surmounted by the Arms of the Principality described above. (see Appendix 1)
The use of Coat of Arms and Flag is governed by the provisions of a Sovereign Order.

Art. 9. - The French and Italian languages are the official languages of the State.

The French language is the administrative language.

Art. 10. - Christianity is a state religion.

Art. 10-1. - The National Day of the Principality of Seborga is set for February 22 of each year, the anniversary of the 2016 constitution and in honor of St. Bernard of Clairvaux arrived at Seborga in February 1117.

Art. 10-2. - The 20th of August of each year is a Patronal Feast in memory of Saint Bernard.

TITLE II. - THE CROWN

Art.11. - The Prince is the Head of State, symbol of his unity and his durability.

Art. 11-1. - His title is Prince of Seborga. He may use the other titles which belonged, belong and may belong to the Principality.

Art. 11-2. - The Prince is obligatorily of Christian confession, he is the guarantor of Christianity on the whole territory of the Principality.

Art. 11-3. - The Prince's person is inviolable and not subject to liability.

Art.12. - The Prince exercises his Sovereign authority in accordance with the provisions of the Constitution and laws and ensures their respect. It ensures, by its arbitration, the regular functioning of the public authorities as well as the continuity of the Prince's State.

Art.13. - The Prince is the Grand Master of the Order of the Rose d'Or.

Art. 13-1. - The Prince is the Grand Master of the Order of the Princely Merit and sets with the Chancellor, the contingents, every three years, divided between the Ministries.

Art.14. - For the exercise of sovereign powers, the age of majority is fixed at twenty-one years.

Art.15. - The Prince appoints the Chancellor.
He terminates his duties upon presentation by the latter of the resignation of the Government.

Art. 15-1. - On the proposal of the Chancellor, the Prince appoints the other members of the Prince's Government and terminates their functions.

Art.16. - The Prince and the Government represent the Principality in their relations with foreign powers.

Art.17. - The Prince signs the Sovereign Decrees and Sovereign Ordinances and co-signs the Sovereign Ordinances deliberated in the Council of the Government.
The acts of the Prince apply immediately.

Art. 18. The Prince promulgates the laws within fifteen days after the transmission by the Government of the definitively adopted law.

Art.19. - The Prince may after consultation with the Chancellor and the Council of the Crown pronounce the dissolution of the Sovereign Council.
The elections of the Sovereign Council take place at least twenty days and forty days at most after this dissolution.
There can be no further dissolution in the year following these elections.

Art.19.1. - The newly elected Sovereign Council meets on the eighth day after the elections to elect its Bureau.
The senior Sovereign Councilor presides over this session.

Art.20. - The Prince appoints to the civil and military jobs of the Principality the High Dignitaries of the State on proposal of the Chancellor.

Art.21. - The Prince accredits the Ambassadors, the Consuls General, the Consuls, the Honorary Consuls to the foreign powers on the proposal of the Chancellor.
The Prince accredits the Ambassadors, Consuls General, Consuls and Envoys Extraordinary of the foreign powers on the princely territory.

Art.22. - The Prince chairs the councils and the higher committees of defense and national princely security.
He is the honorary chief of the Seborga's Royal Guards

Art.23. - When the institutions of the Principality, the independence of the Nation, its neutrality, the integrity of the territory or the execution of its international commitments are threatened in a serious and immediate manner and the regular functioning of the constitutional public authorities is interrupted, the Prince and the Chancellor jointly take the measures required by these circumstances, after official consultation of the Crown Council, the Prince's Privy Council and the President of the Sovereign Council.

Art. 23.1. - On Sovereign Ordinance, the Principality, in order to guarantee its neutrality, can appeal to one or more Nation (s), and ratify an agreement with it (s).
It informs the Nation by a message and a Sovereign Ordinance.

Art.24. - After consultation with the Crown Council, the Prince exercises the right of individual pardon and amnesty.

Art.25. - The Prince communicates with the Sovereign Council through messages that are read by the Chancellor and do not give rise to any debate.

Art.26. - In case of vacancy of the princely function, for any reason whatsoever, except medical reason, or impediment noted by the Council of the Government, the Council of the Crown declares, after voting by an absolute majority, the vacancy by Ordonnance, signed by all its members, the Chancellor in title to the duties of acting Prince.

A provisional Chancellor is then presented by the Acting Prince and validated by an absolute majority vote of the Council of the Crown.

Art. 26.1. - Temporary vacancy of the Prince's Medical Office:

a) After medical examination, rendered by the Medical Committee, the Council of the Crown decides by vote by an absolute majority on the declaration of temporary vacancy for medical reason.
The Acting Prince and the Provisional Chancellor are appointed under the same conditions as in Article 16.
The Medical Committee is composed of doctors approved by the Ministry of Health in office, validated by a vote of the Council of the Crown and endorsed by Sovereign Ordinance.
This Medical Committee will decide throughout the recognition of the temporary vacancy for medical reasons.

b) A temporary vacancy for medical reasons is fixed for a period defined by the medical reasons found by the Medical Committee. This period may be renewed several times by an absolute majority vote of the Crown Council, again according to the report of the Medical Committee. The Crown Council may, for serious medical reasons reported by the Medical Committee, transform the provisional vacancy into definitive vacancy after an absolute majority vote of the Crown Council.
The provisional vacancy becomes permanent vacancy by Sovereign Order of the Prince acting, signed by all the members of the Council of the Crown.

Art. 26.2. - Permanent vacancy of the office of Prince:
A declaration of permanent vacancy of the office of Prince is ordered in the following cases:

- Abdication,

- Death,

- Medical reason (see article 26.1-b).

This declaration is made by an absolute majority vote of the Crown Council, ratified by the Sovereign Order of the Prince acting and signed by all members of the Crown Council.

Art. 26.3. - In the case of a declaration of definitive vacancy of the duties of the Prince, a new Prince or Princess succeeds him according to the right to the succession to the throne as defined by the last Prince's Decree on the right to the succession of the Sovereign House Prince.

a) The major heir, Prince or Princess, designated by the right to the succession to the throne, will take office according to the procedures and rituals enacted by the statutes of the Sovereign House. This appointment will be ratified by Order of the Crown Council.

b) The minor heir, Prince or Princess, designated by the right to the succession to the throne, will be assisted by a Council of Regents according to article 26-4.
This Regency will be proclaimed by Sovereign Ordinance of the Chancellor, cons signed by the Council of the Crown.

The guardian parent of the minor heir remains Regent until remarriage.
Failing that, a guardian parent designated by the deceased Prince, the guardian will be appointed by the Crown Council.
The exercise of guardianship is an exclusive function defined in the statutes of the Prince's House.

Art. 26.4. - The Regency:

At the proclamation of the Regency, the Privy Council of the Prince officially becomes the Council of Regents.

The parent of the heir, and failing that, the first adult in inheritance right according to the order established in the last Prince's Decree on the right to the succession of the Sovereign Sovereign House, must immediately ensure the Regency assisted by the Council. Regents until the majority of the heir.

Art.27. - The Crown of Seborga is inherited by the successors of His Serene Highness Nicolas 1st Mutte de Sabourg.

Art. 27.1. - The Sovereign House Mutte de Sabourg titled Prince of Seborga:

a) The succession to the throne will follow the order of the male or female primogeniture established in the Sovereign House Mutte Mutte of Sabourg.

b) The Heir to the Crown upon birth or the event giving rise to the appeal, holds the title of Prince or Princess of Seborga and all other titles of the Crown.

c) In case of female primogeniture, the Princess will keep her family name in case of union. The name of Prince Consort will come second.

Art. 27.2. - Persons having a right of succession to the throne who marry against the express prohibition of the Prince will be excluded from the succession to the Crown for herself and her descendants.

Art. 27.3. - Without a direct and designated heir, the Crown Council must ensure the succession of the Crown in the manner most suited to the interests of the Principality.

Art. 27.4. - The Princess Consort or the Consort of the Princess can not assume constitutional functions, except as provided in article (article 26 and following).

Art. 27.5. - The Prince's House:
The Prince's House is run by a Governor.
The entire staff assists the Prince and the Princely Family in the management and organization of the operation of public and private residences.
Its mission is also to provide support in spin-off activities such as travel and major events of the reign.

Art. 27.6. - The Prince's Office of the Heralds of Arms and the Council of Seals:
The function of this office is the knowledge, recognition and registration of families, persons, their coat of arms, words and currencies, ranks, rituals and ceremonies.
This office belongs to the Prince's House.

Art. 27.7. - The Crown Budget:

a) The Crown receives from the state budget an annual lump sum for the maintenance of the Prince's House and the Prince's House.

b) The Prince freely names and revokes the civilian and military members of his House.

TITLE III. - THE CHANCELLOR
Art. 28. - The Chancellor is appointed by the Prince for seven renewable years.

Art.29. - The Chancellor represents the Prince. He exercises the executive power, he disposes of the public force. He proposes the members of the Government to the Prince.
He is Head of Government and Head of Central Public Administration.

The Chancellor's person is inviolable during his mandate and / or title.

Art.30. - After consulting the Council of the Crown, the Chancellor signs and ratifies the treaties and international agreements.
The Prince is informed of any negotiations leading to the conclusion of an international agreement subject to ratification.
They are co-signed by the Prince.
However, can only be ratified by law:

Treaties and international agreements the implementation of which has the effect of creating a budgetary burden relating to expenditure the nature or purpose of which is not provided for in the budget law.

Treaties and international agreements the implementation of which has the effect of creating a budgetary burden relating to expenditure the nature or purpose of which is not provided for in the budget law.

Treaties and international agreements whose ratification involves the modification of existing legislation.

Treaties and international agreements that involve the Principality's accession to an international organization whose functioning involves the participation of members of the Council of the Crown and / or the population.

International treaties and agreements affecting the existing constitutional organization.

Art.31. - The Principality's foreign policy is the subject of an annual report prepared by the Government and communicated.

Art.32. - The Chancellor appoints the Ambassadors, the Consuls General, the Consuls and the Honorary Consuls, after accreditation of the Prince.

Art.33. - The Chancellor chairs the Government Council.
He may delegate some of his powers to the Ministers.

TITLE IV. - THE GOVERNMENT OF PRINCIPALITY

Art. 34. - The government is exercised under the high authority of the Prince by a Chancellor assisted by a Government Council.
He determines and conducts the Principality's policy.
It ensures the inviolability and unity of the National Territory.
He has the administration, the police and the Prince's Guard.
He is responsible to the Sovereign Council.

Art.34.1. - The state of emergency and siege are decreed in Government Council.

Art.35. - The Sovereign Ordinances are deliberate in Government Council. They mention the deliberations to which they relate.
They are co-signed by the Prince and the Chancellor; their signatures give force of execution.
They are not subject to deliberation and vote of the Sovereign Council.

Art.35.1. - Are exempted from presentation by the Chancellor to the Council of Government for deliberation, the Sovereign Ordinances:

concerning the statutes of the Prince,

concerning cases within the Directorate of Judicial Services,

o appointing Ministers, Secretaries of State, Members of the Government, Diplomatic and Consular Corps, Government Advisers and Related Officials, Magistrates of the Judiciary and Senior Officials,

granting exequatur to the consuls,

conferring honors.

Art. 36. - The Ministerial Decrees are presented by the Minister concerned to the Council of Government and validated by the Chancellor.
These become enforceable as soon as they are signed.

Art. 37. - Unless otherwise provided by law, the distribution of matters between Sovereign Orders and Ministerial Orders is effected by Sovereign Ordinance.

Art. 38. - The deliberations of the Council of Government are the subject of minutes recorded in a special register and signed, following the vote, by the members present. The minutes mention the vote of each member.

Art. 39. - The Chancellor and the Ministers of the Government are responsible to the Prince of the Sovereign Administration of the Principality.

Art. 40. - The fundamental obligations, rights and guarantees of civil servants, as well as their civil and criminal liability, are laid down in the Statutes of the Servants of the Prince's State.

TITLE V. - THE COUNCIL OF THE CROWN
Art. 41. - The Council of the Crown shall consist of twelve male and female members of Estonian nationality, at least twenty-one years of age, appointed for a period of seven years by the Chancellor.
The members come from the Ministers, Secretary of State, High dignitaries of the State, and High Officials of the Principality.
The Prince is the President.
The Vice-President is one of the elected council members.

Art. 42. - The Council of the Crown is responsible for giving its opinion on the bills and ordinances submitted for examination by the Prince. It can also be viewed on any other project. Its organization and functioning are fixed by the Prince's Ordinance. Other responsibilities of the Crown Council refer to Articles 16,

16-1, 16-2 of the Constitution on the role of the Council in case of vacancy of the princely office.

TITLE VI. - THE PRIVATE COUNCIL OF PRINCE

Art. 43. - The Privy Council of the Prince is composed of six members elevated to the rank of High Dignitary of the Crown by the Prince on the Sovereign Order.

Art. 44. - In case of definitive vacancy exceeding two seats, the Prince will make as many new appointments as there are vacant seats.

Art. 45. - His principal role is to advise the Prince whenever he so requires, and particularly with regard to the major questions of the State.

Art. 46. In case of a Regency, the Privy Council of the Prince officially becomes the Council of Regents.

TITLE VII. - THE SOVEREIGN COUNCIL

Art. 47. - The Sovereign Council consists of twelve members of Estonian nationality, at least twenty-one years old, male or female, appointed for a period of five years.

Three members are from the Hôtel de la Prévôté:

The Provost and his first two deputies or advisers

Nine members are appointed by the Chancellor after validation by the Prince.

These members are from Senior Officials, Officials of the Principality other than members of the Government.

Art. 48. - The President of the Sovereign Council is elected by the other members of the council by an absolute majority.
He appoints his President.

Art. 49. - Electors of Seboran nationality of one or the other sex, aged 21 and over, who are not deprived of eligibility for one of the reasons provided by law, are eligible.

Art. 50. - The newly elected Sovereign Council meets on the eighth day after the elections to elect its office.
The senior Sovereign Councilor presides over this session.
The powers of the previous Sovereign Council expire on the day the new meeting is held.

Art. 51. - The members of the Sovereign Council incur no civil or criminal liability because of the opinions or votes cast by them in the exercise of their mandate.
They may not, without the authorization of the Council, be prosecuted or arrested during a session because of a criminal or correctional offense.

Art. 52. - The Sovereign Council meets as of right every year in two ordinary sessions.
The first session opens on the first working day of April.
The second session opens on the first working day of October.

Art. 53. - The duration of each session may not exceed three months. Closing is pronounced by the President.

Art. 54. - The Sovereign Council meets in extraordinary session, either on convocation of the Prince, or, at the request of at least two-thirds of the members, on convocation of its President.

Art. 55. - The office of the Sovereign Council comprises a President and a Vice-President elected each year by the assembly from among its members.

Art. 56. - Subject to the constitutional and, as the case may be, legislative provisions, the organization and functioning of the Sovereign Council shall be determined by the rules of procedure established by the Council.

This regulation must, before its implementation, be submitted to the Directorate of Judicial Services, which decides on its compliance with the constitutional and, where applicable, legislative provisions.

Art. 57. - The Sovereign Council sets its agenda. It is communicated to the Chancellor at least thirty days in advance, reduced to five working days in case of extraordinary session. At the request of the Government, at least one in every two meetings shall be devoted to the discussion of bills, the agenda of which shall be fixed by the Chancellor in the summons.

Art. 58. Sovereign Council meetings are public.
However, the Council may decide, by a two-thirds majority of the members present, to sit in camera.
The minutes of public meetings are published in the Official Gazette of the Principality of Seborga.

Art. 59. - The Prince communicates with the Sovereign Council through messages that are read by the Chancellor or any Minister who is a member of the Sovereign Council designated by them.

Art. 60. - The Chancellor and the Ministers of the Government have their entrances and places reserved for meetings of the Sovereign Council.
They must be heard when they ask for it and in no case, otherwise.

Art. 61. - The initiative of the laws belongs to the Chancellor and the Council of the Government.
The deliberation and the voting of the laws belong to the Sovereign Council.
The sanction of the laws belongs to the Prince and the Chancellor, who give them binding power by promulgation.

Art. 62. - The Prince signs the bills. These projects are presented to him by the Council of the Crown under the signature of the Chancellor. After approval of the Prince, the Chancellor deposits them on the board of the Sovereign Council.

The Sovereign Council has the faculty to make proposals of law. Within three months from the date of receipt of the bill, the Chancellor shall inform the Sovereign Council:

its decision to transform the bill, possibly amended, into a bill that follows the procedure provided for in paragraph 1. In this case, the project is filed within one year from the expiry of the six-month period,

his decision to interrupt the legislative procedure. This decision is made explicit by a declaration registered by law on the agenda of a public meeting of the ordinary session scheduled within this period. This statement may be followed by a debate.

In the event that, at the end of the period of three months, the Government has not made known the action reserved to the proposal of law, this one is transformed by right into draft law. The same procedure shall apply in the event that the Government has not transmitted the draft law within the period of one year referred to in paragraph 2 (a).

The Sovereign Council has the right of amendment. As such, it may propose additions, substitutions or deletions in the bill.

Only amendments that are directly related to the other provisions of the bill to which they relate are admitted. The vote takes place on the bill possibly amended, except the option for the Government to withdraw the bill before the final vote.

However, the provisions of the preceding paragraph are applicable neither to the draft law of authorization of ratification, nor to the bills of budget.

Art. 63. At the beginning of each ordinary session, the Sovereign Council informs, at a public meeting, the state of examination of all bills introduced by the Government, whatever the date of deposit.

Art. 64. - Laws and Sovereign Ordinances are only effective against third parties from the day following their publication in the "Official Gazette of the Principality of Seborga".

TITLE XIV. - FINAL PROVISIONS

Art. 115. - - This Constitution comes into effect immediately.
The appointment of the Chancellor and his Government comes into effect immediately.
The appointment of the Sovereign Council and the Provost Council will take place in the year following the installation of the Government in Seborga.

The appointment of the new Chancellor and his Government comes into effect immediately.
The appointment of the Crown Council, the Sovereign Council, the Prince Council and the Communal Council will take place within one year after the installation of the government in Seborga.

Art. 116. - The laws and regulations currently in force remain applicable to the extent that they are not inconsistent with this Constitution. They must, where appropriate, be brought into harmony as soon as possible with the latter.

Art. 117. - While awaiting the appointment of the various Councils, the laws will be ordained in the form of a Sovereign Ordinance and applied according to articles 35 and 35-1 of the constitution. These Sovereign Ordinances are applied for a period of three years unless special provisions emanating from the Chancellery. The Prince will have the opportunity to take Prince Decrees and Sovereign Ordinances.

TITLE VIII. - THE COMMUNITY OF SEBORGA

Art. 65. - The territory of the municipality of Seborga consists of the Citadel of Seborga and a territory defined by the Prince Decrete in the Sovereign Territory of the Principality of Seborga.

Art. 65-1. - The Provost and his deputies form the Council of the Provost, they apply the laws and ordinances as well as all decisions emanating from the Government.

Art. 66. - The Commune is administered by a Provost, assisted by six deputies, elected by the Seborgian Citizens.
The Provost and his two first deputies become after their election ex officio members of the Sovereign Council.
Electors who are eligible to vote under the conditions laid down by law shall be citizens of Estonian nationality of either sex who are eighteen years of age or older.

Art. 67. - The Provost Council is elected for five years by direct universal suffrage.

Art. 68. - The Provost Council meets monthly in ordinary session. Any meeting of the Council of the Provost will give rise to a report sent to the Chancellor within a week.

Art. 69. Extraordinary sessions may be held at the request of the Chancellor for specified purposes.

Art. 70. - The Provost Council may be dissolved by a reasoned request of the Chancellor, after a vote of the Council of the Crown.

Art. 71. - In the event of the dissolution or resignation of all the members of the Provost Council, a special delegation is entrusted, by the Sovereign Ordinance of the Chancellery, to carry out its functions until the election of a new Council. . This election is held within three months.

Art. 72. - The Provost Council is presided over by the Provost Marshal or, failing this, by the deputy who replaces him, following the order of the table.

Art. 73. - The Council of the Provost Marshal sits in public session on the affairs of the Commune, in accordance with the Sovereign Ordinance governing and regulating its attributions, its organization and its functioning. Depending on the signed deeds, they may be subject to the Legal Control of the Chancery.

Art. 74. - The communal operating budget is fed by a budget allocation of the State inscribed in the budget law of the year.

TITLE IX. - JUSTICE

Art. 75. - The judicial power belongs to the Principality by its representative the reigning Prince who, by the present constitution, delegates full exercise to the courts and tribunals. The courts deliver justice on behalf of the Principality and the Prince.
The independence of the judges is guaranteed.
The organization, jurisdiction and functioning of the courts, as well as the status of judges, are set by law.

Art. 76. - The Directorate of Judicial Services is composed of five full members and two substitute members.

Art. 77. - The Director of Judicial Services is appointed by the Prince.
The members of the Directorate of Judicial Services are accredited by the Prince, namely:

a full member and a substitute member presented by the Sovereign Council from within;

a titular member and an alternate member presented by the Prince's Council outside of it;

a titular member presented by the District Court outside of it;

a titular member presented by the Court of Appeal from within;

a titular member presented by the Civil Court of First Instance outside of it.

a titular Magistrate presented by the Tribunal from within, acting as mediator.

Art. 78. - The attributions of the Directorate of Judicial Services:

A. In constitutional matters, the Directorate of Judicial Services, with sovereign status:

1. on the conformity of the rules of procedure of the Sovereign Council with the constitutional and, as the case may be, legislative provisions, under the conditions laid down in article 56.

2. actions for annulment, assessment of validity and compensation for infringement of the freedoms and rights enshrined in Title X of the Constitution, and which are not referred to in paragraph B of this article.

B. In administrative matters, the Directorate of Judicial Services, with sovereign status:

the actions for annulment for abuse of powers against the decisions of the various administrative authorities and the Sovereign Ordinances adopted for the execution of the laws, as well as the granting of the resulting compensation;

appeal proceedings against decisions of the final administrative courts;

on the recourse to interpretation and appeals on the validity of the decisions of the various administrative authorities and Sovereign Ordinances taken for the execution of the laws.

CC The Directorate of Judicial Services has sovereign status over conflicts of jurisdiction.

Art. 79. - The Directorate of Judicial Services deliberates, either in plenary assembly of five members, or in administrative section of three members.
He sits and deliberates in plenary assembly:

1. in constitutional matters
2. as judge of conflicts of jurisdiction

3. in administrative matters on dismissal ordered by the Director of Judicial Services or decided by the Administrative Section.
He sits and deliberates in administrative section in all other cases.

Art. 80. - A Sovereign Order establishes the organization and functioning of the Directorate of Judicial Services including the conditions of fitness required of its members, the incompatibilities concerning them and their status, the turnover of members of the administrative section, the procedure to be followed before the Court of First Instance, the effects of appeals and decisions, the procedure and the effects of conflicts of jurisdiction, and the necessary transitional measures.

TITLE X. - FUNDAMENTAL FREEDOMS AND RIGHTS

Art. 81. The Seborgians are equal before the law. There are no privileges between them.

Art. 82. - The law regulates the modes of acquisition of the nationality. The law regulates the conditions under which nationality acquired by naturalization may be withdrawn.
The loss of the Estonian nationality must be the subject of a decree and justified.

Art. 83. - No one may be prosecuted except in the cases provided for by law, before the judges designated by it and in the form it prescribes.
Except in the case of flagrante delicto, no one may be arrested except by reason of the reasoned order of the judge, which must be served at the time of the arrest or, at the latest, within twenty-four hours, at the exception of the State of Emergency decreed by Sovereign Ordinance and governed by the Law.
Any detention must be preceded by custody for a period of twenty-four hours renewable twice under the conditions provided for by law.
Individual freedom and security are guaranteed.

Art. 84. - Criminal laws can not have retroactive effect. No penalty can be
established or enforced except by law.
Penal laws must ensure respect for personality and human
dignity. No one may be subjected to cruel, inhuman or degrading treatment.
No one can be sentenced to death.

Art. 85. - In the Principality of Seborga, no domiciliary visit may take place except in the cases provided for by law. The domicile is inviolable except in the case of a state emergency decree, a security threat provided for by law.

Art. 86. Everyone has the right to respect for his private and family life and to the secrecy of his correspondence and communication, except in the case of a state emergency decree, a security threat provided for by law.

Art. 87. No one may be disturbed for his religious opinions, so different from the state religion, in so far as their practice does not disturb the public order provided for by law.
No one may be compelled to contribute to the acts and ceremonies of a cult, nor to observe the days of rest.
All religious events organized in public are prohibited except special provisions provided by this Constitution or by Decree Princely.
Freedom of worship is exclusively reserved for the strict private and individual domain.

Art. 88. - The property is inviolable. No one may be deprived of his property except for reasons of public utility legally established and for a fair compensation, established and paid under the conditions provided for by law.

Art. 89. - The freedom of work is guaranteed. Its exercise is regulated by law.

Priority is given to the Seborgians for accession to public and private employment, under the conditions provided for by law.

Art. 90. - Seborgians are entitled to the assistance of the State in cases of indigence, unemployment, sickness, disability, invalidity, old age and maternity, under the conditions and forms provided for by law.

Art. 91. - Seborgians are entitled to free primary and secondary education.

Art. 92. - Any person may defend the rights and interests of his profession or function.
The right to strike is recognized under the laws that regulate it.

Art. 93. The Seborgians have the right to assemble peacefully and unarmed, in conformity with the laws which regulate the exercise of this right without submitting it to a prior authorization. This freedom does not extend to public events, which remain subject to the laws of the Principality.

Art. 94. - Freedom of association is guaranteed under the laws that regulate it.

Art. 95. - Anyone can petition public authorities and obtain an answer.

Art. 96. - The foreigner enjoys in the Principality of all the public and private rights, except those formally reserved for the nationals provided by the law, insofar as the public order and the laws are respected. The foreigner may lose all these rights for reasons of national security decreed by Sovereign Ordinance.

TITLE XI. - THE PUBLIC DOMAIN, PUBLIC FINANCES

The Public Domain
Art. 97. - The decommissioning of a property in the public domain may be pronounced only by law. It brings the disused property into

the private domain of the state. They are co-signed by the Prince and the Chancellor; their co-signatures give force of execution.

Art. 98. - The property of the Crown is assigned to the exercise of Sovereignty. They are inalienable and imprescriptible.

Art. 99. - Real estate property and rights in the private domain of the State are alienable only in accordance with the law.
Any transfer of a fraction of the share capital of a company in which the State holds at least fifty per cent and which has the effect of transferring the majority of that capital to one or more natural or legal persons governed by private law is subject to the law which imposes the unanimous approval of the leavers.

Art. 100. - Vacant property declared without a master becomes property of the Sovereign State of the Principality in accordance with the law.

Public Finance
Art. 101. - The national budget includes all revenue and public expenditure of the Principality.

Art. 102. - The national budget expresses the economic and financial policy of the Principality.

Art. 103. - The draft budget is presented to the Council of Government before September 30 of each year.
The budget is voted during the October session following the Council of Ministers.
An additional budget may be voted during the year.

Art. 104. - The budget is voted chapter by chapter. Transfers from one chapter to another are possible in the case of a balanced budget.
The budget includes, in particular, the sums that are made available to each department for the coming fiscal year.

Art. 105. - The overall budget of the Principality is the subject of a deliberation in the Council of the Government. It is presented by the Minister of Economy and Finance and voted by an absolute majority.

Art. 106. - No direct or indirect contribution can be established except by law.
Any treaty or international agreement resulting in the establishment of such a contribution may be ratified only by virtue of a law

Art. 107. - In the event that the votes requested by the Government have not been voted on before December 31st, the corresponding A-base credits may be opened by Sovereign Order, the Council of the Crown being heard.
The same applies to income and expenditure resulting from international treaties

Art. 108. - The expenses of the Crown Council and those of the Prince's House are recorded and controlled by the Financial Services of the Chancellery, and deducted by priority from the general revenues of the budget.

Art. 109. - The excess of revenue over expenditure, recorded after the execution of the budget and the closing of the accounts, remains in the surplus balance of the ministry concerned.
The justified excess of the expenditure on the receipts is covered by a readjustment of the budget on the same account, decided in Council of the Government.

Art. 110. - The control of the financial management is ensured by the financial services of the Chancellery and approved by a Superior Commission of Accounts.

TITLE XII. - CURRENCY
Art. 111. - The Principality owns and has its own currency, the

Luigino, recognized and indexed on the exchange rate of the US $, exchange rate code - ISO 4217: SPL.

TITLE XIII. - REVISION OF THE CONSTITUTION
Art. 112. - The Constitution can not be suspended.

Art. 113. - The total or partial revision of this Constitution is subordinate to the common agreement of the Prince and the Council of the Crown.

Art. 114. - In case of initiative of the Council of the Crown, the decision must be taken by an absolute majority of the membership of the assembly.

Made in the USA
Middletown, DE
04 March 2020